Workbook

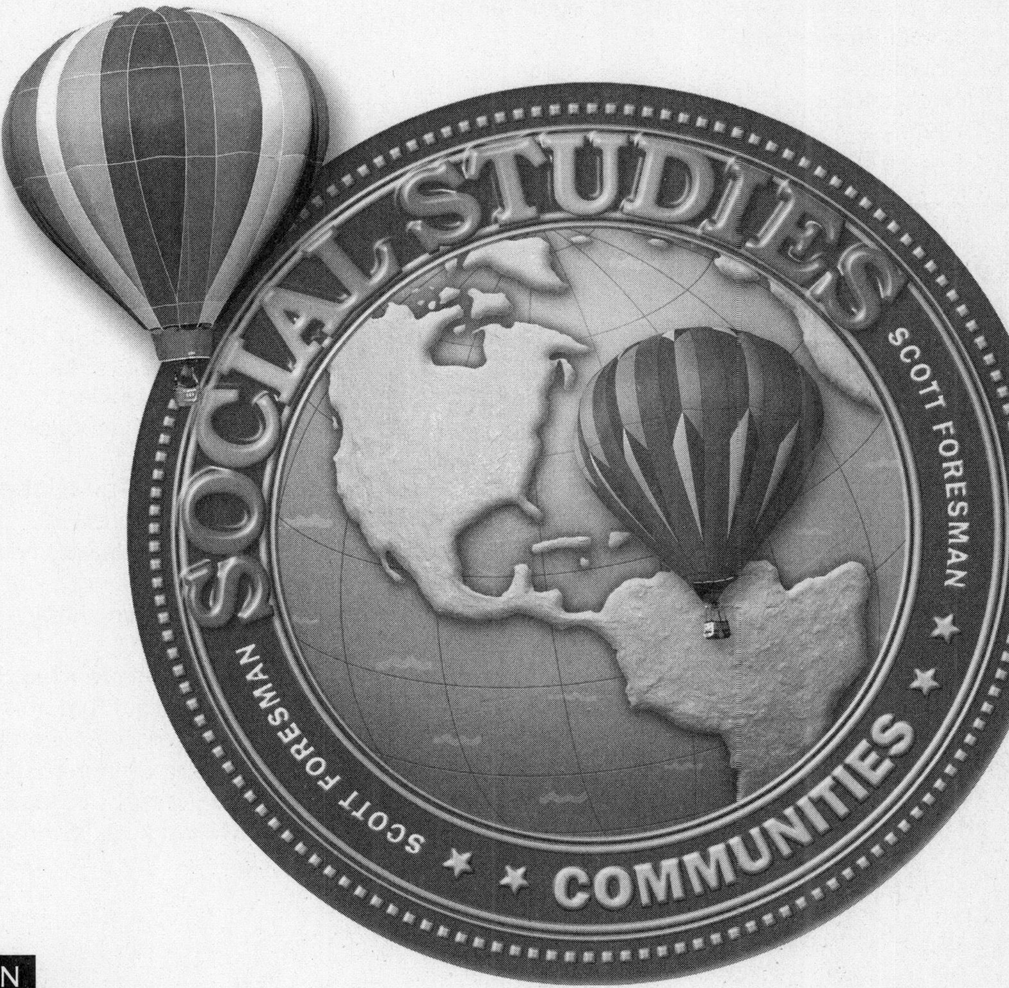

PEARSON
Scott Foresman

Editorial Offices: Glenview, Illinois • Parsippany, New Jersey • New York, New York
Sales Offices: Parsippany, New Jersey • Duluth, Georgia • Glenview, Illinois • Coppell, Texas • Ontario, California • Mesa, Arizona

www.sfsocialstudies.com

Program Authors

Dr. Candy Dawson Boyd
Professor, School of Education
Director of Reading Programs
St. Mary's College
Moraga, California

Dr. Geneva Gay
Professor of Education
University of Washington
Seattle, Washington

Rita Geiger
Director of Social Studies and
  Foreign Languages
Norman Public Schools
Norman, Oklahoma

Dr. James B. Kracht
Associate Dean for
  Undergraduate Programs
  and Teacher Education
College of Education
Texas A&M University
College Station, Texas

Dr. Valerie Ooka Pang
Professor of Teacher Education
San Diego State University
San Diego, California

Dr. C. Frederick Risinger
Director, Professional
  Development and Social
  Studies Education
Indiana University
Bloomington, Indiana

Sara Miranda Sanchez
Elementary and Early
  Childhood Curriculum
  Coordinator
Albuquerque Public Schools
Albuquerque, New Mexico

Contributing Authors

Dr. Carol Berkin
Professor of History
Baruch College and the
  Graduate Center
The City University of New York
New York, New York

Lee A. Chase
Staff Development Specialist
Chesterfield County
  Public Schools
Chesterfield County, Virginia

Dr. Jim Cummins
Professor of Curriculum
Ontario Institute for Studies
  in Education
University of Toronto
Toronto, Canada

Dr. Allen D. Glenn
Professor and Dean Emeritus
Curriculum and Instruction
College of Education
University of Washington
Seattle, Washington

Dr. Carole L. Hahn
Professor, Educational Studies
Emory University
Atlanta, Georgia

Dr. M. Gail Hickey
Professor of Education
Indiana University-Purdue
  University
Fort Wayne, Indiana

Dr. Bonnie Meszaros
Associate Director
Center for Economic Education
  and Entrepreneurship
University of Delaware
Newark, Delaware

ISBN 0-328-08176-0

Copyright © Pearson Education, Inc.
All rights reserved. Printed in the United States of America. The blackline masters in this publication are designed for use with appropriate equipment to reproduce copies for classroom use only. Scott Foresman grants permission to classroom teachers to reproduce from these masters.

17 18 19 20 -V0N4- 14 13 12 11

Contents

Unit 1: Our Community

Chapter 1
- Reading Social Studies 1
- Vocabulary Preview 2
- Lesson 1 Review 3
- Lesson 2 Review 4
- Lesson 3 Review 5
- Map and Globe Skills 6
- Vocabulary Review 7

Chapter 2
- Vocabulary Preview 8
- Lesson 1 Review 9
- Lesson 2 Review 10
- Lesson 3 Review 11
- Thinking Skills 12
- Vocabulary Review 13
- Discovery Channel Project 14

Unit 2: People in Communities

Chapter 3
- Reading Social Studies 15
- Vocabulary Preview 16
- Lesson 1 Review 17
- Lesson 2 Review 18
- Lesson 3 Review 19
- Lesson 4 Review 20
- Map and Globe Skills 21
- Vocabulary Review 22

Chapter 4
- Vocabulary Preview 23
- Lesson 1 Review 24
- Map and Globe Skills 25
- Lesson 2 Review 26
- Lesson 3 Review 27
- Vocabulary Review 28
- Discovery Channel Project 29

Unit 3: Where Are Communities?

Chapter 5
- Reading Social Studies 30
- Vocabulary Preview 31
- Lesson 1 Review 32
- Lesson 2 Review 33
- Chart and Graph Skills 34
- Lesson 3 Review 35
- Vocabulary Review 36

Chapter 6
- Vocabulary Preview 37
- Lesson 1 Review 38
- Lesson 2 Review 39
- Research and Writing Skills 40
- Lesson 3 Review 41
- Vocabulary Review 42
- Discovery Channel Project 43

Unit 4: History of Communities

Chapter 7
Reading Social Studies 44
Vocabulary Preview 45
Lesson 1 Review 46
Research and Writing Skills 47
Lesson 2 Review 48
Map and Globe Skills 49
Lesson 3 Review 50
Lesson 4 Review 51
Vocabulary Review 52

Chapter 8
Vocabulary Preview 53
Lesson 1 Review 54
Chart and Graph Skills 55
Lesson 2 Review 56
Lesson 3 Review 57
Writing Prompt 58
Lesson 4 Review 59
Thinking Skills 60
Vocabulary Review 61
Discovery Channel Project 62

Unit 5: Communities at Work

Chapter 9
Reading Social Studies 63
Vocabulary Preview 64
Lesson 1 Review 65
Writing Prompt 66
Lesson 2 Review 67
Thinking Skills 68
Lesson 3 Review 69
Vocabulary Review 70

Chapter 10
Vocabulary Preview 71
Lesson 1 Review 72
Chart and Graph Skills 73
Lesson 2 Review 74
Lesson 3 Review 75
Vocabulary Review 76
Discovery Channel Project 77

Unit 6: Governments

Chapter 11
Reading Social Studies 78
Vocabulary Preview 79
Lesson 1 Review 80
Thinking Skills 81
Lesson 2 Review 82
Writing Prompt 83
Lesson 3 Review 84
Vocabulary Review 85

Chapter 12
Vocabulary Preview 86
Lesson 1 Review 87
Map and Globe Skills 88
Lesson 2 Review 89
Lesson 3 Review 90
Vocabulary Review 91
Discovery Channel Project 92

Name _____ Date _____

 **Reading Social Studies**
Use with Pages 6–7.

Main Idea and Details

Directions: The main idea is the most important idea of a paragraph. Supporting details tell more about the main idea. Read the paragraph. Fill in the circle next to the correct answer.

Even though Hope, Arkansas, is a small community, there are many exciting things to do there. The biggest event held in Hope is the Watermelon Festival. Each year, in August, thousands of people come to enjoy music, food, and games. They also come to see watermelons that weigh between 150 and 200 pounds! Another fun thing to do in Hope is to watch the high school band. The Hope Superband is known all over the state of Arkansas for its music and costumes. Swimming at Fair Park and watching concerts at Klipsch Auditorium are also a lot of fun. A visit to Hope, Arkansas, can be very busy with these activities and more!

1. What is the main idea of the paragraph?
   Ⓐ Another fun thing to do in Hope is to watch the high school band.
   Ⓑ Even though Hope, Arkansas, is a small community, there are many exciting things to do there.
   Ⓒ People come to see watermelons that weigh between 150 and 200 pounds!
   Ⓓ The Hope Superband is known all over the state of Arkansas for its music and costumes.

2. What is NOT an exciting thing people do in Hope, Arkansas?
   Ⓐ go to the Watermelon Festival
   Ⓑ watch the Hope Superband
   Ⓒ eat at Joe's Seafood Shack
   Ⓓ swim at Fair Park

 **Notes for Home:** Your child learned to identify the main idea and supporting details of a paragraph.
Home Activity: Read a story with your child. Ask your child to point out the main ideas and then to identify the supporting facts and details.

Name _____ Date _____

Vocabulary Preview
Use with Chapter 1.

Vocabulary Preview

Directions: These are the vocabulary words from Chapter 1. How much do you know about these words? Draw a line from each word to its meaning. You may use your glossary.

Column A

1. community
2. geography
3. location
4. culture

Column B

a. a place where people live, work, and have fun together

b. the way a group of people lives

c. where something can be found

d. the study of Earth and how people live on it

Now use each of the vocabulary words in a sentence to talk about where *you* live. Write your sentences on the lines below.

5. _____

6. _____

7. _____

8. _____

Notes for Home: Your child learned new terms related to communities.
Home Activity: With your child, skim the community section of a local newspaper. Analyze how the terms *community, geography, location,* and *culture* are used in context.

2 Vocabulary Preview

Workbook

Name _____ Date _____

Lesson Review
Use with Pages 10–15.

Lesson 1: Communities

Directions: A *community* is a place where people live, work, and have fun together. El Paso, Texas, is the community where Carlos lives. Use the terms in the box to complete each sentence with information from Lesson 1. You may use your textbook.

vote	"the pass"	Native Americans	river
Texas	celebrations	United States of America	Mexico

1. El Paso is Spanish for _____.

2. El Paso is located on the border between _____ and the United States.

3. The people in Carlos's neighborhood gather for _____.

4. The first people to live in El Paso were _____.

5. The Rio Grande is a _____ that separates El Paso from Juarez, Mexico.

6. El Paso is located in the state of _____.

7. Texas is one of the states in the _____.

8. Carlos's parents _____ for people who want to help their community.

Notes for Home: Your child learned about the community of El Paso, Texas.
Home Activity: Have your child share how your community is similar to or different from El Paso.

Name _____ Date _____

Lesson Review
Use with Pages 18–23.

Lesson 2: United States Communities

Directions: There are many types of communities in the United States. Use the information from Lesson 2 to fill in the chart about three communities in our country. You may use your textbook.

	It Is Located in the State of:	Its First Settlers Were:	Some Fun Things to Do Are:
Astoria			
Wilmington			
Denver			

Notes for Home: Your child has learned about three communities, each in a different part of the United States.
Home Activity: Locate these three communities on a map. Then have your child locate your community.

Name _____ Date _____

Lesson Review
Use with Pages 26–29.

Lesson 3: World Communities

Directions: There are many types of communities around the world. Some are much like your community. Others are very different! Fill in the squares below with words that tell about the culture of Timbuktu. You may use your textbook. Then fill in the boxes with information about your own culture.

Language	
Timbuktu	
My Community	

Entertainment	
Timbuktu	
My Community	

CULTURE

Clothing	
Timbuktu	
My Community	

Religion	
Timbuktu	
My Community	

Notes for Home: Your child has learned about Timbuktu, in Mali.
Home Activity: Ask your child to compare the culture of Timbuktu with that of your community.

Workbook

Lesson Review **5**

Name _____ Date _____

Map and Globe Skills
Use with Pages 32–33.

Use Map Scales

Directions: Read the map and answer the questions that follow.

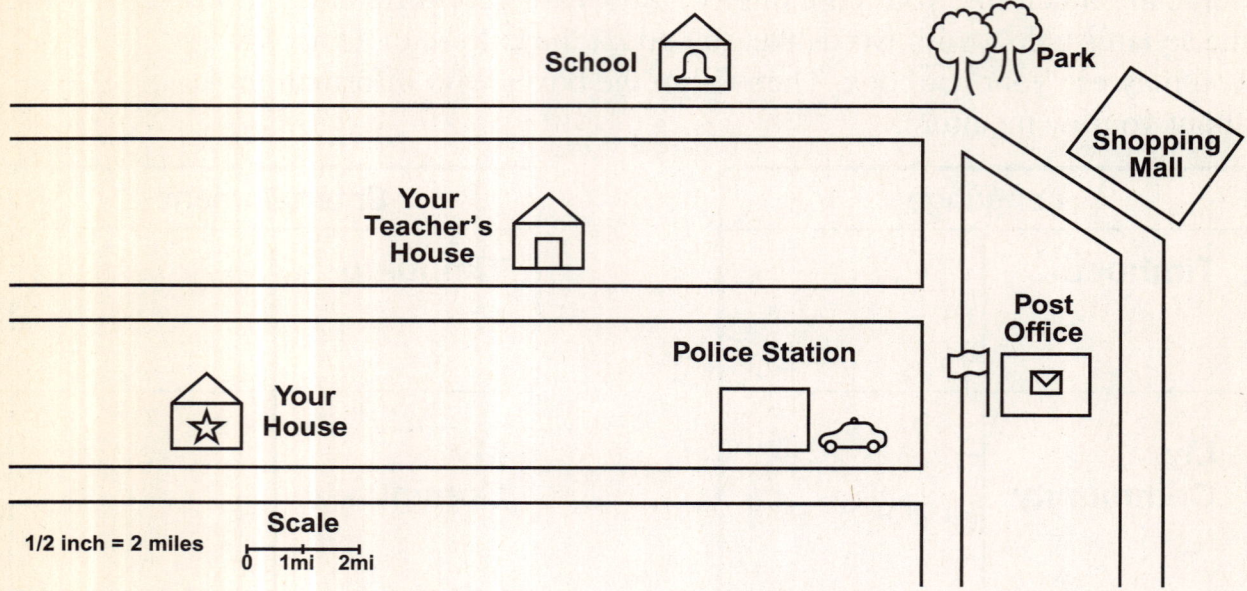

1. How far is it in inches from the school to the park? in miles?

   _____

2. How many miles would you have to walk to get from the park to the shopping mall? _____

3. Would you rather walk or ride a bus from the mall to your teacher's house?

   _____

   _____

4. Suppose that you are planning a 10-mile walk to raise money for your community. Mark on the map the route walkers could take starting from the police station. Where does the walk end?

   _____

Notes for Home: Your child learned how to use a map scale.
Home Activity: Ask your child to measure the distance on the map between a house and the police station, in inches, and then convert to miles.

6 Lesson Review   Map and Globe Skills

Name _____ Date _____

Vocabulary Review

Use with Chapter 1.

Vocabulary Review

Directions: Write each vocabulary word from Chapter 1 beside its examples or description. Then write a letter to someone in another community. Use each word in your letter to tell about where you live.

| community | geography | location | culture |

_____ 1. El Paso, Astoria, Wilmington, Denver, Timbuktu

_____ 2. between two mountains, near a sea, in a desert

_____ 3. spicy food, French language, special holidays

_____ 4. land around a place

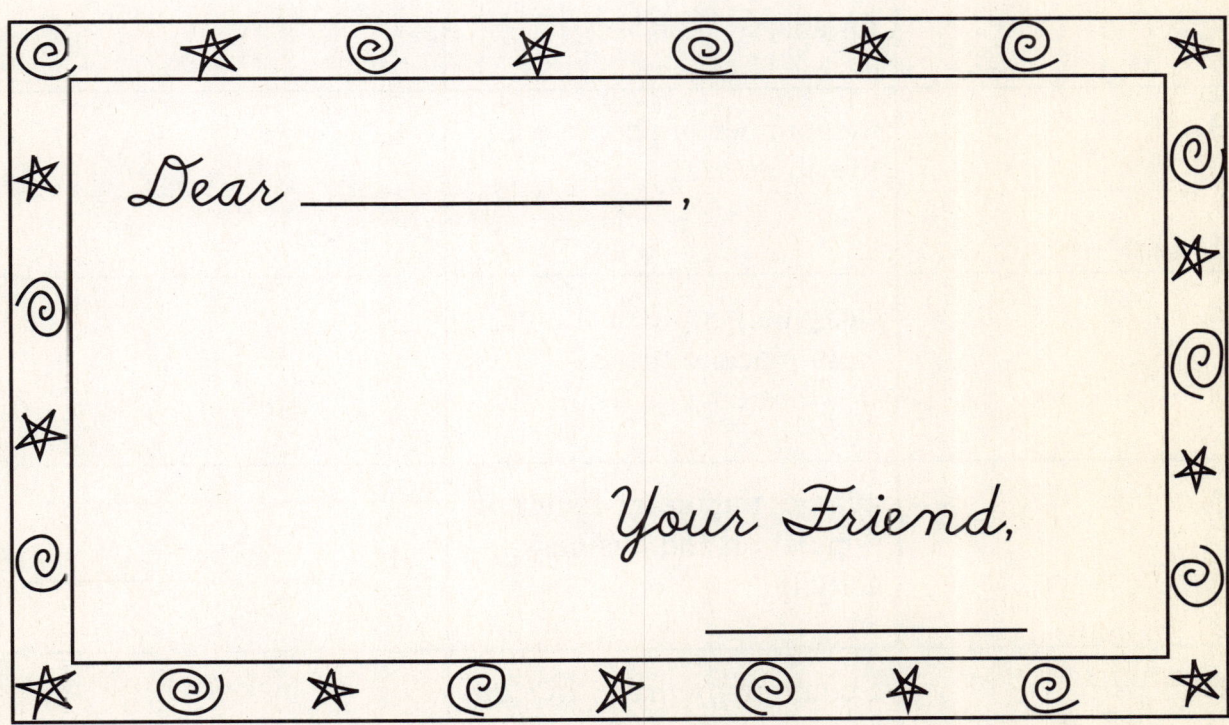

Notes for Home: Your child learned to apply new terms related to communities.
Home Activity: Have your child use the words *community, geography, location,* and *culture* to describe the community in this chapter he or she most wants to visit.

Workbook   **Vocabulary Review**   **7**

Name _____ Date _____

Vocabulary Preview

Use with Chapter 2.

Vocabulary Preview

Directions: These are the vocabulary words from Chapter 2. How much do you know about these words? Write each word in the chart next to its meaning. Then draw an example of each word. You may use your glossary.

| rural community | urban community | population |
| suburban community | city | transportation |

Vocabulary Word	Meaning	Example
1.	a community that is located near a large city	
2.	in the countryside where the towns are small and far apart	
3.	the number of people who live in an area	
4.	carrying people or things from place to place	
5.	a large, important center of population and business activity	
6.	a community that is in a city	

Notes for Home: Your child learned the characteristics of urban, suburban, and rural communities.
Home Activity: Scan the travel section of a Sunday newspaper with your child. Look for examples of each term above.

8 Vocabulary Preview

Workbook

© Scott Foresman 3

Name _____ Date _____

Lesson Review
Use with Pages 38–41.

Lesson 1: A Rural Community

Directions: In a *rural community* the towns are small and far apart. Answer the questions below about life in a rural community. You may use your textbook.

1. Describe where the community of Bridgewater is located.

   _____
   _____
   _____
   _____

2. Where do many of the people who live in Bridgewater work?

   _____
   _____

3. What can you do for fun in Bridgewater?

   _____
   _____

4. Would you like to live in Bridgewater? Why or why not? Give two reasons.

   _____
   _____
   _____
   _____

Notes for Home: Your child learned about the rural community of Bridgewater, Virginia.
Home Activity: With your child, discuss how daily activities in rural communities are the same or different from yours.

Workbook | Lesson Review 9

Name _____ Date _____

Lesson Review
Use with Pages 42–45.

Lesson 2: A Suburban Community

Directions: A *suburban community* is near a large city. How are suburban and rural communities alike? Fill in the shaded part of the Venn diagram with two things that Bridgewater and Levittown have in common. How are Amy's and Steve's communities different? Complete the diagram to show how each one is different. You may use your textbook.

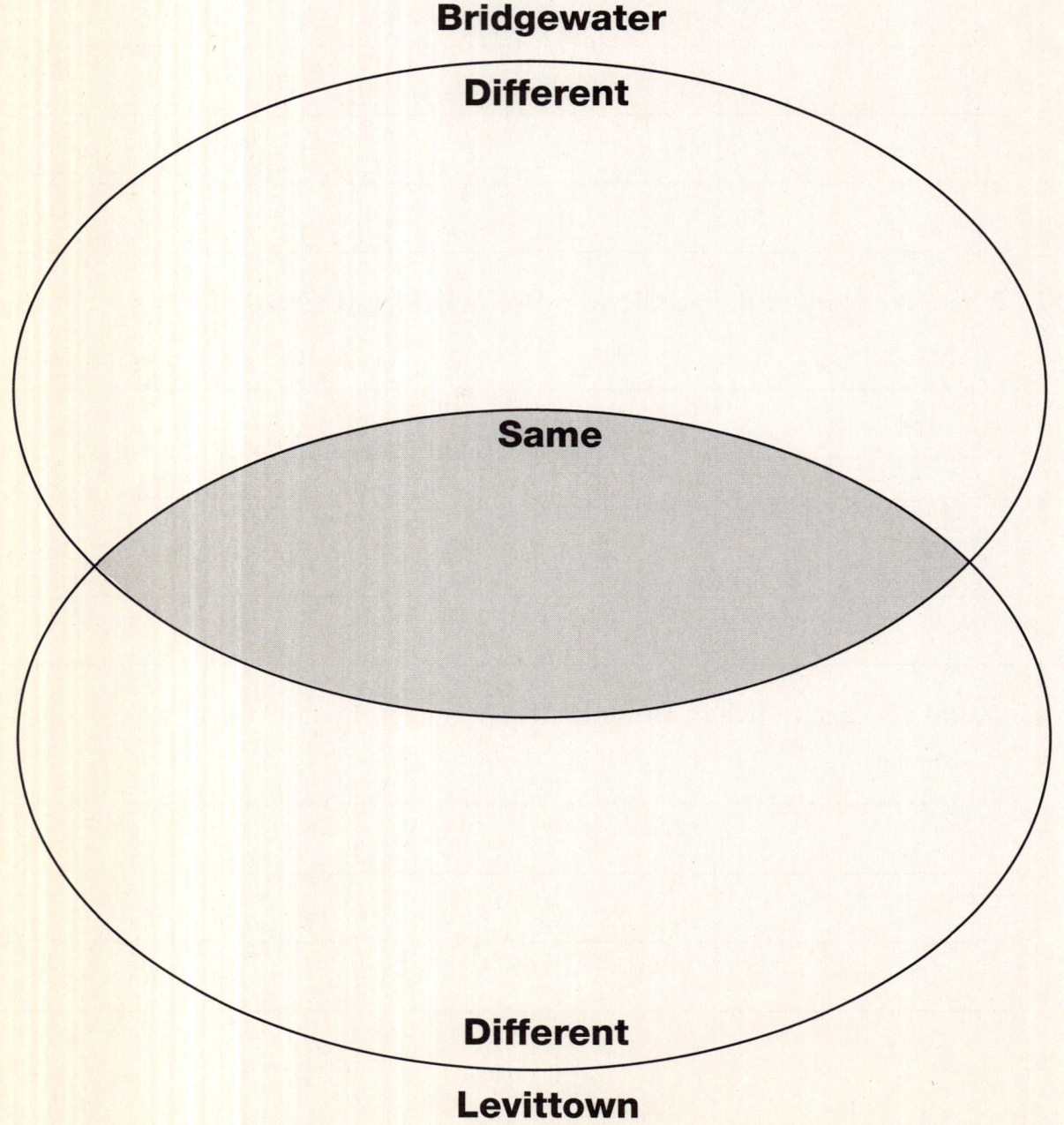

Notes for Home: Your child learned about the suburban community of Levittown, New York.
Home Activity: With your child, discuss what suburban communities are like. Have your child name suburbs near where you live.

Name _____ Date _____

Lesson Review
Use with Pages 48–53.

Lesson 3: An Urban Community

Directions: *An urban community* is in a city with many people. Chicago is the urban community where Beth lives. Suppose you are going to write an article for your school paper about Chicago. Begin preparing for your article by answering these questions. You may use your textbook.

1. WHERE is Chicago located? _____
_____
_____

2. WHO first settled there? _____
WHEN? _____

3. WHEN did Chicago get its name? _____

4. WHERE do people in Chicago work? _____
_____
_____

5. HOW do people get around Chicago? _____
_____

6. WHAT fun things are there to do in Chicago? _____
_____
_____

Notes for Home: Your child learned about the urban community of Chicago, Illinois.
Home Activity: With your child, review the three lessons in this chapter. Ask your child to tell you how urban, suburban, and rural communities are the same or different.

Name _____ Date _____

Thinking Skills
Use with Pages 56–57.

Classify

Directions: You learned about Bridgewater, Levittown, and Chicago in this chapter. Classifying the features of those communities can help you see how they are alike or different. Read the features in the box below. Classify them by writing each feature in the correct place on the chart. Then draw a picture of each community.

in the countryside	in a city	near a large city
Chicago, Illinois	Levittown, New York	Bridgewater, Virginia
people work here or in the city	everyone knows each other	large population
open lands and fields	highways help them grow	many tall buildings

Classify into Group	Features	Looks Like This
Rural community		
Suburban community		
Urban community		

Notes for Home: Your child learned to classify different kinds of communities.
Home Activity: Use pictures of communities from books or magazines and have your child classify the pictures by the type of community each represents.

Name _____ Date _____

Vocabulary Review

Use with Chapter 2.

Vocabulary Review

Directions: Use the clues from the chapter to complete the crossword puzzle.

rural	urban
suburban	population
city	transportation

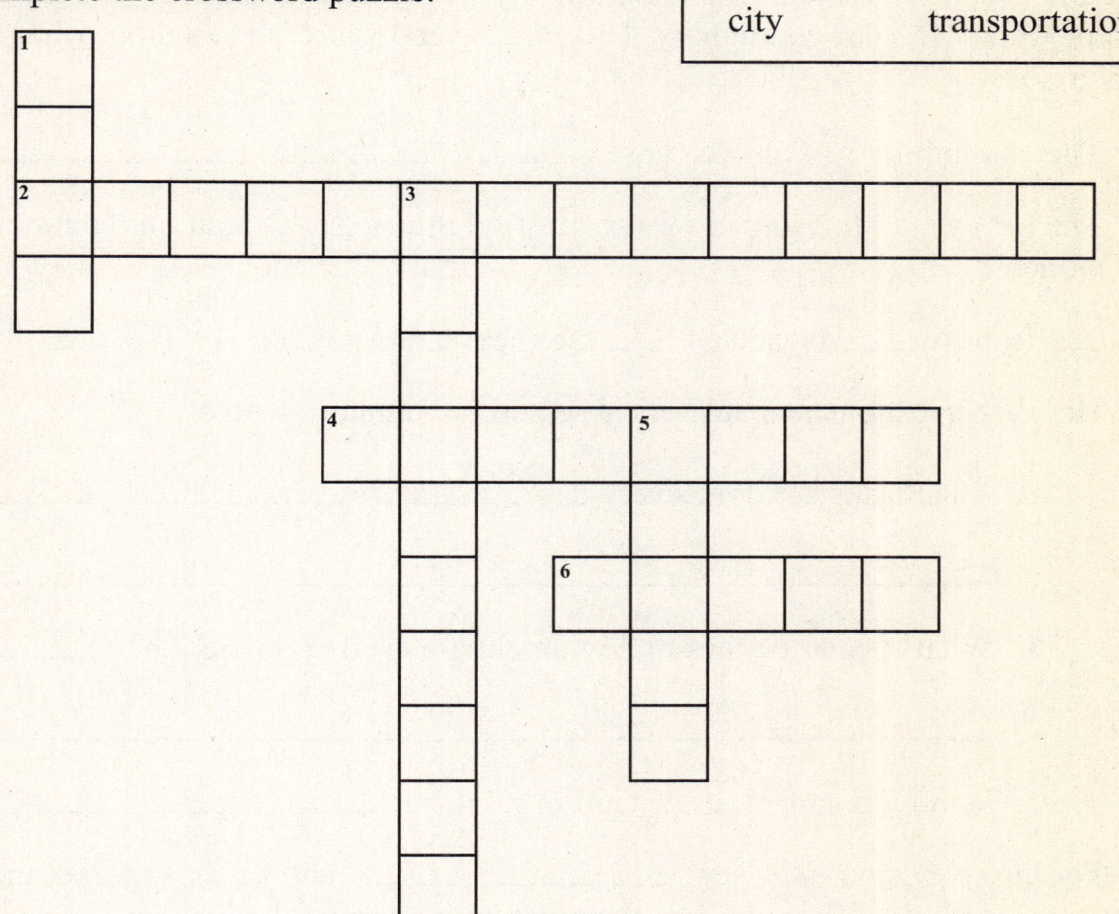

Across

2. carrying people or things from place to place
4. a community that is near a large city, such as Levittown
6. a community that is in a city

Down

1. a large, important center of business activity with a large population, such as Chicago
3. the number of people who live in a place
5. a community in the countryside where the towns are small and far apart

 Notes for Home: Your child learned new terms related to communities.
Home Activity: Have your child name his or her favorite book. Then use each word above in a summary of that story.

Workbook

Vocabulary Review 13

Name _____ Date _____

Use with Page 64.

Unit 1 Project Working in My Community

Plan a television interview with a community worker. With a partner, choose one kind of worker in your community. Then use several sources to find out what that worker does.

1. The community worker we chose is _____.

2. The (✔) shows the source we used to find information about our community worker:

   ____ Books   ____ Magazines   ____ Internet   ____ An adult

3. Here are questions and answers about our community worker:

   A. What tasks are done every day? _____
   _____

   B. What special clothes or equipment are used to do the job? _____
   _____

   C. Is the job dangerous or hard to learn? _____

4. For our television interview, _____ will be the reporter and _____ will be the community worker.

✔ **Checklist for Students**

_____ We chose a community worker.
_____ We found information about our community worker.
_____ We answered questions about our community worker.
_____ We shared what we learned by performing a television interview.

Notes for Home: Your child learned about community workers.
Home Activity: With your child, make a chart of community workers and the goods and services they provide to members of your community.

14 Discovery Channel Project   Workbook

Name _____ Date _____

Use with Pages 70–71.

Compare and Contrast

Directions: When you compare and contrast two things, you tell how they are alike or different. Read the Venn diagram below. It compares and contrasts living in Haiti and living in the United States. Fill in the circle next to the correct answer.

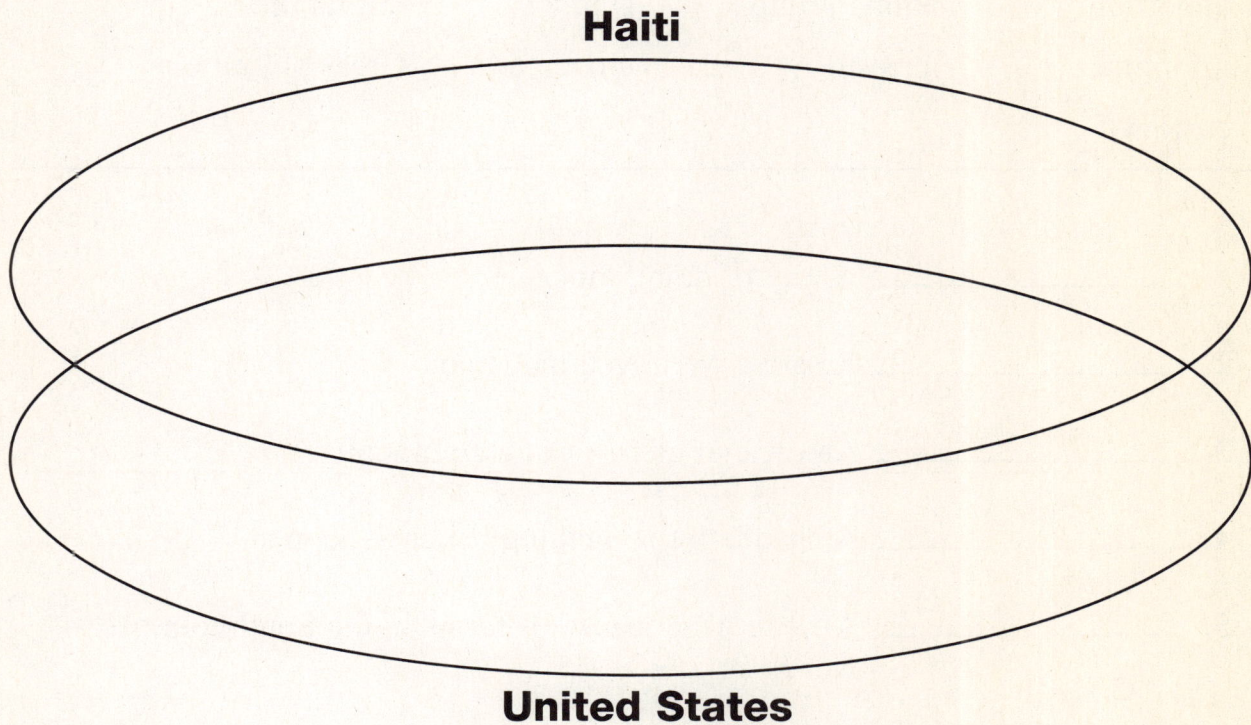

1. How is living in the United States like living in Haiti?

    Ⓐ The weather is warm all the time.
    Ⓑ Everyone speaks Haitian Creole.
    Ⓒ Children go to school.
    Ⓓ English is the official language.

2. How is living in the United States different from living in Haiti?

    Ⓐ Children go to school.
    Ⓑ Some cities get snow in the winter.
    Ⓒ Friends play together.
    Ⓓ People help each other.

Notes for Home: Your child learned to interpret a Venn diagram to compare and contrast.
Home Activity: Discuss with your child the similarities and differences between being a child and being an adult.

Workbook   Reading Social Studies   **15**

Name _____ Date _____

Vocabulary Preview
Use with Chapter 3.

Vocabulary Preview

Directions: These are the vocabulary words from Chapter 3. How much do you know about these words? Write each word on the line beside its definition. You may use your glossary.

opportunity	ethnic group	symbol	migration
immigrant	ancestor	citizen	Great Migration
custom			

1. _____ A way of doing things

2. _____ Relative who lived long ago

3. _____ An official member of a community

4. _____ A chance for something better to happen

5. _____ African Americans left farms in the South to move North for jobs

6. _____ A person who moves into a country and lives there

7. _____ Moving from one part of a country to live in another part

8. _____ Group of people who have the same culture

9. _____ An object that represents something else

Notes for Home: Your child learned the vocabulary terms for Chapter 3.
Home Activity: Discuss with your child your family's ancestors. Share who they were, how they lived, and any memories you have.

Name _____ Date _____

Lesson Review
Use with Pages 74–77.

Lesson 1: Moving to a New Community

Directions: Moving to a new community can be very exciting. There are people to meet and new places to explore. Complete the chart with information from this lesson. You may use your textbook.

People in Tom's Class Move From?	Why Do People Move?	What Do People Do in Their New Community?

Notes for Home: Your child learned about moving to a new community.
Home Activity: Have you or your child ever lived in another community? Discuss with your child the exciting and the difficult things about moving into a new community.

Name _____ Date _____

Lesson Review
Use with Pages 78–81.

Lesson 2: Learning New Customs

Directions: A *custom* is a way of doing things. People in different communities often have different customs. Circle the term in parentheses that best completes each sentence. You may use your textbook.

1. Nicole moved to (Boston, the Caribbean Sea) from Haiti.

2. Nicole's family can still follow some (customs, neighborhoods) from Haiti.

3. Members of the Haitian ethnic group share the same (school, culture).

4. Haiti is a (country, state) in the Caribbean Sea.

5. In Nicole's (immigrant, ethnic) neighborhood, people can speak in their home language.

6. Nicole's family moved to a neighborhood where many other (immigrants, customs) live.

7. Nicole's new friends are helping her learn to speak (Haitian Creole, English).

8. Nicole's family has found (customs, stores) in Boston that sell the foods they like to eat.

9. Nicole's new neighborhood is (different from, exactly like) where she lived in Haiti.

10. Nicole is a part of a Haitian (ethnic group, language).

Notes for Home: Your child learned about adapting to the customs of a new community and maintaining the customs of a home country.
Home Activity: Discuss some of the customs of your family's ethnic group. For example, what languages do you speak? What types of food do you like to eat?

18 Lesson Review Workbook

Name _____ Date _____

Lesson Review
Use with Pages 84–89.

Lesson 3: Where Did They Come From?

Directions: Categorize the words in the box by writing each term on the lines in the correct column. You may use your textbook.

Germany	Boston	writer	*The Promised Land*
12 years old	Russia	painter	9 years old
Philadelphia	*Washington Crossing the Delaware*		

Mary Antin   Emanuel Gottlieb Leutze

_____   _____

_____   _____

_____   _____

_____   _____

_____   _____

Directions: Write a paragraph comparing and contrasting Mary Antin with Emanuel Gottlieb Leutze.

_____

_____

_____

_____

_____

Notes for Home: Your child learned about some of the men and women who immigrated to America and became artists.
Home Activity: Discuss with your child what might prompt people to share their experiences through artwork or writing.

Workbook   Lesson Review

Name _____ Date _____

Lesson Review
Use with Pages 90–95.

Lesson 4: A New Life in America

Directions: People have come from many places to live in the United States. Suppose it is the early 1900s. You have just moved to the United States. Write a letter to a friend in your native country. Tell your friend all about your new home. Be sure to include where you live, what new things you have had to learn, what you have seen, and what types of people you have met. You may use your textbook.

Dear _____,

_____

_____

_____

_____

_____

_____

_____

_____

Your friend,

_____

Notes for Home: Your child learned about immigrants in the early 1900s.
Home Activity: Discuss with your child where your family's ancestors moved from. What problems do you think they faced in their new home?

Name _____ Date _____

Map and Globe Skills
Use with Pages 98–99.

Use Intermediate Directions

Directions: Use what you learned about intermediate directions to answer the questions below the map.

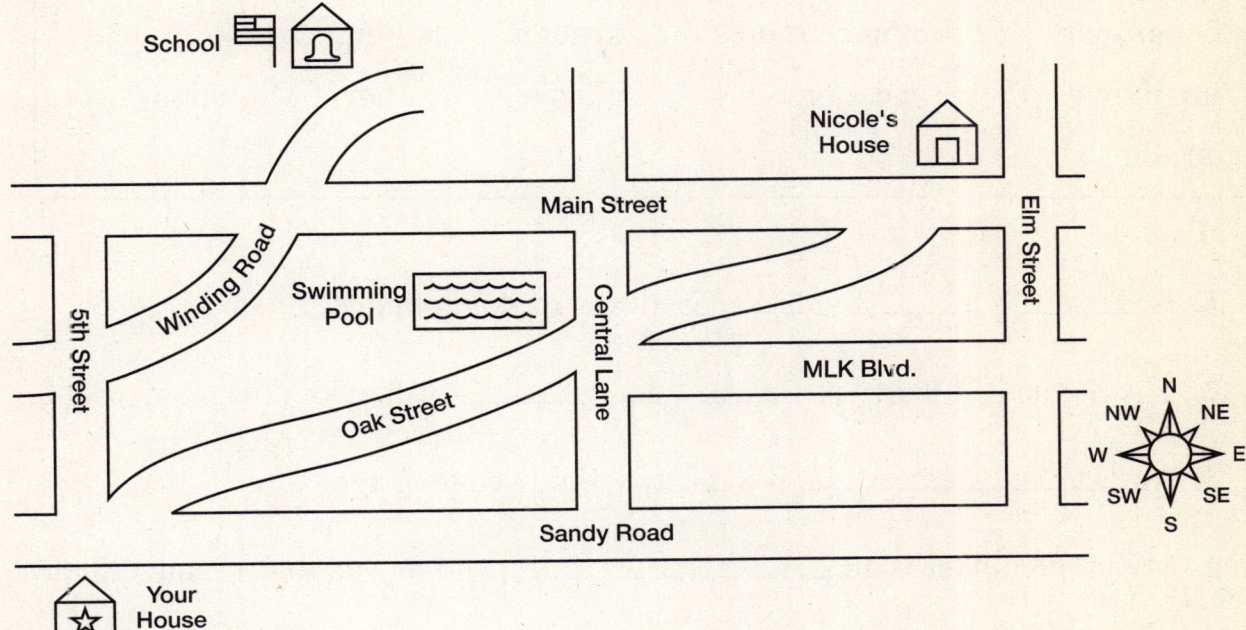

1. Start at your house. Go north on 5th Street. Then go northeast on Winding Road, past Main Street. Where are you headed? _____

2. From there, go southwest on Winding Road and go east on Main Street. What is the name of the first street you come to? _____

3. From your house, in which direction is the swimming pool? _____

4. Nicole, a new student in your class, lives at the corner of Main Street and Elm Street. Explain how your new friend would get to your house. Use intermediate directions.

_____

Notes for Home: Your child learned how to use intermediate directions to follow a map.
Home Activity: On your next trip out of the house, talk about the intermediate directions (northwest, northeast, southwest, southeast) in which you are traveling.

Workbook   Map and Globe Skills **21**

Name _____ Date _____

Vocabulary Review

Use with Chapter 3.

Vocabulary Review

Directions: Choose the vocabulary word from the box that best completes each sentence. Write each word on the line provided.

opportunity	ethnic group	symbol	migration
immigrant	ancestor	citizen	Great Migration
custom			

1. A _____ is a special way of doing things.

2. The Statue of Liberty is a _____ of freedom for many people.

3. An _____ is a relative who lived long ago.

4. My grandmother is an _____ who moved to the United States from Poland.

5. During the _____, many African Americans moved to the North from small farms in the South.

6. Many people move to a new city because of an _____ for a good job.

7. In the United States, a _____ has the right to vote.

8. When people move from one part of a country to live in another part, it is called _____.

9. Nicole is part of a Haitian _____.

Notes for Home: Your child learned the vocabulary terms for Chapter 3.
Home Activity: Talk about your family history with your child. Use as many of the vocabulary words from this chapter as you can in your discussion.

Name _____ Date _____

Vocabulary Preview

Use with Chapter 4.

Vocabulary Preview

Directions: These are the vocabulary words from Chapter 4. How much do you know about these words? Use the vocabulary words to complete the crossword puzzle. You may use your glossary.

| holiday | tradition | livestock | Civil Rights Movement |

Across

2. a drive for change that fought for fair treatment of all Americans

4. animals raised on farms

Down

1. a special day for remembering an important person or event

3. a special way that a group does something

Notes for Home: Your child learned the vocabulary terms for Chapter 4.
Home Activity: Your child already may be familiar with the terms *holiday* and *tradition*. Discuss examples of each.

Workbook

Vocabulary Preview **23**

Name _____ Date _____

Lesson Review

Use with Pages 104–109.

Lesson 1: Celebrating Cultures

Directions: Families all over the world celebrate their special holidays. Complete the chart with traditions that are a part of the holidays listed. In the last row of the chart, write your favorite holiday and some of your family's traditions for that holiday. Then answer the questions that follow. You may use your textbook.

Holiday	Traditions
Asian New Year	
Christmas	
Hanukkah	
Kwanzaa	
Eid-al-Fitr	
Cinco de Mayo	
St. Patrick's Day	
My favorite holiday is: _____	

1. What are two religious holidays shown in the chart?

   _____

   _____

2. What does the Cinco de Mayo holiday celebrate?

   _____

Notes for Home: Your child learned that celebrations are a part of many cultures.
Home Activity: Discuss your child's favorite holiday. What is your favorite holiday? Why? Discuss with your child the traditions of that holiday.

24 Lesson Review   Workbook

Name _____ Date _____

Map and Globe Skills
Use with Pages 110–111.

Understand Hemispheres

Directions: Dividing Earth into hemispheres gives you an easy way to locate places. Use your textbook to find the continents listed below. On the lines provided, write in which hemispheres that continent is located. Remember that each continent can be found in either the Northern or Southern Hemisphere **and** the Eastern or Western Hemisphere.

	Northern or Southern?	**Eastern or Western?**
1. Africa	_____	_____
2. Asia	_____	_____
3. Australia	_____	_____
4. Europe	_____	_____
5. North America	_____	_____
6. South America	_____	_____

Directions: On the lines provided, explain how one place can be located in either the Northern or Southern Hemisphere *and* the Eastern or Western Hemisphere.

_____

_____

_____

Notes for Home: Your child learned how to find a place on a map or globe according to its hemispheres.
Home Activity: Use a map or globe to find the United States. Discuss with your child in which hemispheres it is located. Find your family's country or countries of origin. In what hemispheres are those countries located?

Workbook   Map and Globe Skills **25**

Name _____ Date _____

Lesson Review
Use with Pages 114–117.

Lesson 2: Celebrating a Community's Past

Directions: Many communities hold special celebrations, such as festivals and fairs, to celebrate their history. Use complete sentences to answer questions 1–5. You may use your textbook.

1. Why do some communities hold a Founders Day?

   _____
   _____

2. What does the heritage festival in New Orleans honor?

   _____
   _____

3. What do state fairs celebrate?

   _____
   _____

4. What are some of the things people bring to display at the fair in Hutchinson, Kansas?

   _____
   _____
   _____

5. What does the Green Corn Festival celebrate?

   _____
   _____
   _____

Notes for Home: Your child learned how communities come together to celebrate their past.
Home Activity: Discuss a celebration your community holds. What is the purpose of the celebration or whom does it honor?

Name _____ Date _____

Lesson Review
Use with Pages 120–123.

Lesson 3: Celebrations Across Our Nation

Directions: Some holidays are celebrated by communities all across the United States. Use the terms in the box to complete each sentence with information from Lesson 3. You may use your textbook.

harvest	United States	equally	Wampanoag Indians
January	freedom	England	Civil Rights Movement
Monday	Memorial Day	Pilgrims	Thanksgiving Day

1. _____ is a national holiday honoring people who served in the _____ armed forces. We celebrate it on the last _____ in May.

2. Martin Luther King, Jr., Day is celebrated on the third Monday in _____. It also remembers a fight for _____. Dr. King led a drive called the _____. He fought for all people to be treated _____.

3. _____ is celebrated with a special meal. Today we give thanks like the _____, who had come from _____, because they wanted to be free to practice their religion. They first gave thanks in 1621 for their good _____. They also thanked the _____ who welcomed them and helped them.

Notes for Home: Your child learned how communities across the United States celebrate three special holidays.
Home Activity: Discuss with your child the concepts of freedom, fairness, and thankfulness. Talk about why they are important to your family, your community, and the country.

Workbook   Lesson Review **27**

Name _____ Date _____

Vocabulary Review

Use with Chapter 4.

Vocabulary Review

Directions: Write each vocabulary word from Chapter 4 beside its definition. Then use each word in a sentence.

| holiday | tradition | livestock | Civil Rights Movement |

1. _____ animals raised on farms

   _____

   _____

2. _____ a special way that a group does something

   _____

   _____

   _____

3. _____ a special day for remembering an important person or event

   _____

   _____

   _____

4. _____ a drive for equal treatment of all citizens

   _____

   _____

   _____

Notes for Home: Your child learned the vocabulary terms for Chapter 4.
Home Activity: Take turns with your child using each of the vocabulary terms from Chapter 4 in a sentence.

Name _____ Date _____

Unit 2 Project Celebrate!

Use with Page 132.

Directions: In a group, give a news report about an event or celebration in your community. Choose someone to play the role of TV news reporter.

1. The group chose _____ to play the TV news reporter.

2. The community event or celebration is _____.

3. Here are questions and answers about our event or celebration.

   A. Why do we celebrate this event? _____
   _____

   B. How long ago did our community begin holding this celebration?
   _____

   C. When does the event take place? _____
   _____

   D. What decorations, costumes, or special foods are part of the celebration?
   _____

✔ Checklist for Students

_____ We chose a community event or celebration.
_____ We chose a group member to be the TV news reporter.
_____ We wrote answers to questions about the event or celebration.
_____ We presented our television news report to the class.

Notes for Home: Your child learned about community celebrations.
Home Activity: With your child, discuss your favorite community event or celebration. Share details about the event, reasons for celebrating it, and why you enjoy it.

Workbook   Discovery Channel Project **29**

Name _____ Date _____

Reading Social Studies

Use with Pages 138–139.

Draw Conclusions

Directions: A conclusion is a decision or opinion you make after you think about some facts and details. Read each fact. Then answer the question that follows. Fill in the circle next to the correct answer.

1. Tonya likes to go boating and fishing. She also likes to watch alligators. What conclusion can you draw about where Tonya lives?

    Ⓐ She lives in a desert.
    Ⓑ She lives near water, such as a river or lake.
    Ⓒ It rains and snows a lot where she lives.
    Ⓓ She lives where many trees and flowers grow.

2. Winona lives in a region where very little rain falls. She likes to take photographs of the cactuses and snakes near her house. What conclusion can you draw about cactuses and snakes?

    Ⓐ They like to swim in rivers.
    Ⓑ They need to live in a place with a lot of snow.
    Ⓒ They do not like to be photographed.
    Ⓓ They do not need much water to live.

3. Nick lives in Omaha, Nebraska. He likes to ride his bike on the flat paths around his town. What conclusion can you draw about the physical environment around Omaha?

    Ⓐ There are not many hills or mountains around Omaha.
    Ⓑ There are swamps with alligators and Spanish moss around Omaha.
    Ⓒ There are deserts and cactuses around Omaha.
    Ⓓ There are hills and forests around Omaha.

Notes for Home: Your child learned to draw conclusions from a set of facts.
Home Activity: Discuss with your child what you can see and do in and around your community. Help your child draw conclusions about your community's physical environment.

Name _____ Date _____

Vocabulary Preview

Use with Chapter 5.

Vocabulary Preview

Directions: These are the vocabulary words from Chapter 5. How much do you know about these words? Write the number of each word on the line before its meaning. You may use your glossary.

1. region
2. physical environment
3. climate
4. landform
5. ecosystem
6. adapt
7. adobe
8. natural resource
9. mineral
10. fuel
11. conserve
12. recycle

_____ a. a shape on the Earth's surface

_____ b. a mixture of earth, straw, and water that is formed into bricks and dried

_____ c. a substance that can be burned to produce heat, light, or other forms of energy

_____ d. a natural resource that has never been alive

_____ e. the kind of weather a place has from year to year

_____ f. the landforms and climate of a region

_____ g. to use resources carefully

_____ h. to change the way you do something

_____ i. to use something again

_____ j. a large land area that has special features

_____ k. a useful material that comes from the earth

_____ l. a physical environment and all the living things in it

Notes for Home: Your child learned the vocabulary terms for Chapter 5.
Home Activity: To practice these terms in context, discuss with your child the climate and landforms of your community.

Workbook

Name _____ Date _____

Lesson Review

Use with Pages 142–147.

Lesson 1: What Is Your Community's Environment?

Directions: The physical environment of a community helps make it a special place. Complete the chart with information from this lesson. You may use your textbook.

	Western Region	Northeast Region	Southeast Region	Midwest Region	Southwest Region
What is one community in this region?					
What landforms can you see there?					
What plants and animals can you see there?					
What fun things can you do there?					

Notes for Home: Your child learned about the five physical regions of the United States.
Home Activity: Have your child identify in which region of the country you live. Discuss the landforms, plants, and animals of your community.

Name _____ Date _____

Lesson Review
Use with Pages 150–155.

Lesson 2: Living in Different Climates

Directions: The United States is a country with many different climates. Answer the following questions about the climate in each of these communities. You may use your textbook.

1. **Barrow, Alaska**

   Describe its climate. _____

   What causes its climate to be like that? _____

   _____

2. **Kauai, Hawaii**

   Describe its climate. _____

   What causes its climate to be like that? _____

   _____

3. **Cape Cod, Massachusetts**

   Describe its climate. _____

   What causes its climate to be like that? _____

   _____

4. **Omaha, Nebraska**

   Describe its climate. _____

   What causes its climate to be like that? _____

   _____

5. **Your community**

   Describe its climate. _____

© Scott Foresman 3

Notes for Home: Your child learned about the many climates in the United States and how location and physical environment affect a community's climate.
Home Activity: Discuss with your child the climate of your community. How do location and environment affect its climate?

Workbook • Lesson Review **33**

Name _____ Date _____

Chart and Graph Skills

Use with Pages 158–159.

Use a Line Graph

Directions: The line graph below shows how the average monthly snowfall in Helena, Montana, changes over a six-month period. Read the line graph and answer the questions that follow.

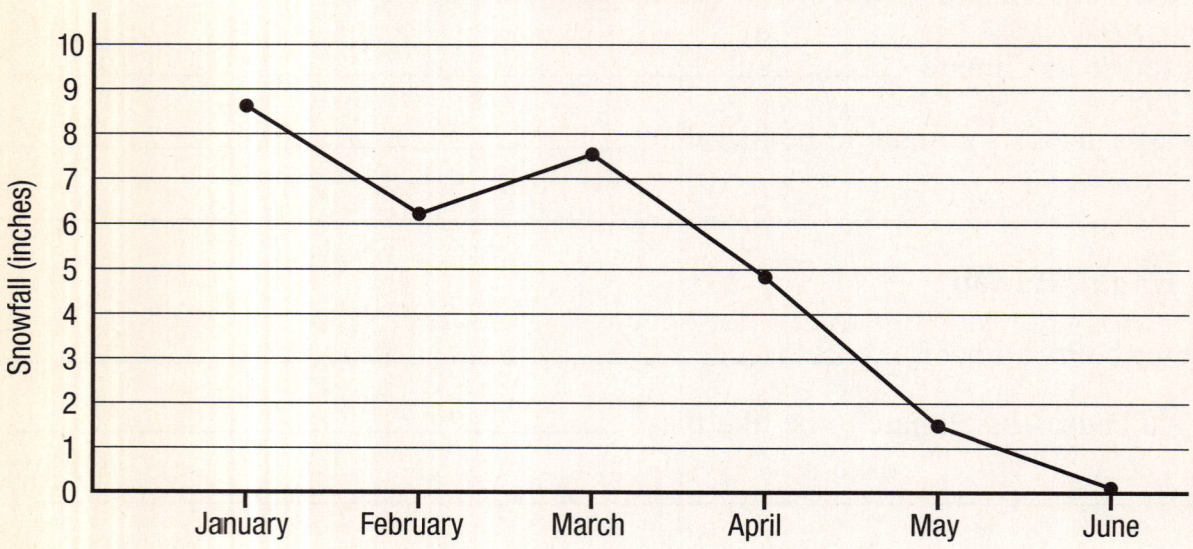

1. What is the title of the graph?

   _____

2. Between which two months does the amount of snowfall change the most?

   _____

3. Between which two months does the amount of snowfall go up?

   _____

4. Look at the monthly changes in the graph. How much snow do you think falls in July? _____

Notes for Home: Your child learned how to interpret line graphs.
Home Activity: With your child, watch, listen to, or read weather reports for your community over the course of a week. Plot the daily high temperatures on a line graph with your child.

Name _____ Date _____

Lesson Review
Use with Pages 160–165.

Lesson 3: Communities and Resources

Directions: Natural resources are useful materials that come from the earth. The natural resources found in a community help it grow. Circle the term in parentheses that best completes each sentence. You may use your textbook.

1. A mineral is a natural resource that has (never, always) been alive.

2. Gold and (salt, trees) are minerals.

3. Oil and gas are types of (crops, fuels).

4. Gas can be burned to produce (food and drink, heat and light).

5. Two very important natural resources are water and (climate, soil).

6. In 1848, gold was discovered in what is now (Nebraska, California).

7. The movement west to look for gold is known as the (Gold Rush, Civil Rights Movement).

8. People dug deep (mines, lakes) where they found gold and brought it to the surface.

9. California is called the (Golden State, Angels Camp) because of its sunny days and the gold that brought people there.

10. (Oil, Gold) is a valuable resource that was found in Beaumont, Texas.

11. Another name for oil is "(liquid, black) gold."

12. The population of Beaumont (grew quickly, stayed the same) when oil was found.

13. Texas and (Connecticut, Alaska) are two top oil-producing states.

14. We (conserve, change) resources when we use them carefully.

15. We can conserve natural resources by using less of them and by (mining, recycling) them.

Notes for Home: Your child learned about the value of natural resources to a community.
Home Activity: What natural resources are in your area? With your child, find out what they are, where they are found, and how they have contributed to the history and economy of your community.

Workbook   Lesson Review **35**

Name _____ Date _____

Vocabulary Review

Use with Chapter 5.

Vocabulary Review

Directions: Choose the vocabulary word from the box that best completes each sentence. Write the word on the line provided. Not all words will be used.

region	landform	adobe	fuel
physical environment	ecosystem	natural resources	conserve
climate	adapt	mineral	recycle

1. Some of the valuable _____ found in the United States are soil, water, oil, and gold.

2. Bozeman, Montana, is in the Western _____ of the United States.

3. A _____ can be burned to produce energy.

4. A region's _____ includes its landforms and climate.

5. A _____ is a natural resource that has never been alive.

6. One way to _____ natural resources is to use less of them.

7. People _____ to living in cold places by heating their buildings and wearing warm clothing.

8. The Pueblo have adapted to the climate in Taos by building houses made of _____.

Directions: Choose two of the vocabulary words not used above. Use each one in a sentence. Write your sentences on the lines that follow.

_____

_____

_____

Notes for Home: Your child learned the vocabulary terms for Chapter 5.
Home Activity: Help your child apply these vocabulary words by using them in a conversation with you.

Name _____ Date _____

Vocabulary Preview
Use with Chapter 6.

Vocabulary Preview

Directions: Match each vocabulary word to its meaning. Write the vocabulary word on the line before the definition. You may use your glossary.

miner	port	state government
logging	industries	crossroads
lumber	state capital	

1. _____ wood that is cut into boards so it can be used for building

2. _____ a city in which the state government is located

3. _____ a place where ships can load and unload things

4. _____ a place where many different roads meet one another

5. _____ people who make the state's laws

6. _____ a person who digs materials from the earth

7. _____ kinds of businesses

8. _____ cutting down trees to use for wood

Directions: Use three of the vocabulary words in sentences to describe your community. Write your sentences on the lines below.

9. _____

10. _____

11. _____

Notes for Home: Your child learned the vocabulary terms for Chapter 6.
Home Activity: Discuss your state and local governments with your child. Who is your governor? mayor? Where is your state capital?

Workbook   Vocabulary Preview **37**

Name _____ Date _____

Lesson Review
Use with Pages 172–175.

Lesson 1: A Mountain Community

Directions: The resources found in mountain areas can help a community grow. The events in the box are a part of the history of the mountain community of Glenwood Springs, Colorado. Write the events in the order they happened. Some dates have been provided. You may use your textbook.

Captain Cooper and others set up Fort Defiance.

Miners came to dig coal.

The town's name was changed to Glenwood Springs.

The Colorado Midland Railroad came to town.

Other settlers came to enjoy the hot springs.

Ute Indians discovered hot water springs in Glenwood Canyon.

↓

1879:

↓

↓

1881:

↓

↓

Notes for Home: Your child learned the sequence of the major events in the history of a mountain community: Glenwood Springs, Colorado.
Home Activity: What has happened in Glenwood Springs since 1887? Review this lesson with your child. Add other events to the "time line."

Name _____ Date _____

Lesson Review
Use with Pages 178–181.

Lesson 2: A Water Community

Directions: Lakes, rivers, and other bodies of water can provide communities with many resources. Seattle, Washington, is a community near an ocean. Read the descriptions of people, things, and places from Seattle's history in the chart below. Complete the chart with information from this lesson. You may use your textbook.

Who?	1. _____	One group of Indians who lived near the town
	_____	Another group of Indians who lived near the town
	2. _____	Indian leader for whom Seattle is named
	3. _____	People who cut down trees
What?	4. _____	Three natural resources of the Seattle area
	5. _____	One important business in Seattle
	6. _____	One main use for wood
	7. _____ and _____ Two new industries that have come to Seattle	
Where?	8. _____	The location where settlers built their town
	9. _____	The large body of water near Seattle
	10. _____	A place where ships load and unload things

Notes for Home: Your child learned about the history of a community near the water: Seattle, Washington.
Home Activity: Discuss water pollution with your child. Help him or her think of ways to educate other children about the problem.

Name _____ Date _____

Thinking Skills

Use with Pages 184–185.

Use Conflict Resolution

Directions: Conflict sometimes happens at school. Two people may want to use the same book at the same time. A few students may disagree about who is first in line. Identify a conflict that could happen at school, and describe what can be done to resolve the conflict.

1. What is the conflict? _____
   _____

2. What should the people in conflict do to find a solution?
   _____
   _____

3. Who can be a mediator for the conflict?
   _____
   _____

4. What is a possible compromise or solution for the conflict?
   _____
   _____

Notes for Home: Your child learned how to use conflict resolution.
Home Activity: Scan a section of the newspaper with your child. Work together to identify and resolve a conflict from one of the news articles.

Name _____ Date _____

Lesson Review
Use with Pages 186–189.

Lesson 3: A Crossroads Community

Directions: Some communities are built at a crossroads, or a place where many different roads come together. The community of Indianapolis, Indiana, is known as the "Crossroads of America." Fill in the chart below with 8 facts about Indianapolis. You may use your textbook.

_____   _____

_____   _____

_____   _____

_____   _____

Notes for Home: Your child learned about the history of a crossroads community: Indianapolis, Indiana.
Home Activity: Discuss with your child the types of transportation that can be seen in your community.

Workbook   Lesson Review **41**

Name _____ Date _____

Vocabulary Review

Vocabulary Review
Use with Chapter 6.

Direction: Write each vocabulary word from Chapter 6 on the lines below its definition. Then write each letter marked with a star in the spaces provided in question 9. These letters will form a new word that answers the question.

1. a city in which the state government is located

   _ _ _ _   _ _ _ _ _ _
            *

2. a place where ships can load and unload things

   _ _ _
     *

3. wood that is cut into boards so it can be used for building

   _ _ _ _ _
       *

4. a person who digs materials from the earth

   _ _ _ _ _
   *

5. cutting down trees to use for wood

   _ _ _ _ _ _ _
           *

6. kinds of businesses

   _ _ _ _ _ _ _ _ _ _
           *

7. people who make the state's laws

   _ _ _ _   _ _ _ _ _ _ _ _ _
       *

8. a place where many different roads meet one another

   _ _ _ _ _ _ _ _ _
         *

9. What can be found in the mountains, near water, or at a crossroads of transportation? _ _ _ _ u _ i _ i _ _
                                     1 2 3 4 5 6 7 8

Notes for Home: Your child learned the vocabulary terms for Chapter 6.
Home Activity: Take turns with your child using each of the vocabulary words from Chapter 6 in a sentence.

Name _____ Date _____

Use with Page 198.

Unit 3 Project Use and Reuse

Directions: Make a product with reused materials. Then make an advertisement to sell your product. Present your completed product and advertisement to the class.

1. My product is a _____

   made from a used _____.

2. I used these additional materials to make my product:

   _____   _____

   _____   _____

   _____   _____

3. I made an advertisement to sell my product. Each (✓) below shows what I included in my advertisement:

   ____ product name

   ____ picture of the product

   ____ what materials I reused to create the product

   ____ directions on how to use the product

   ____ price

✓ Checklist for Students

_____ I made a product with reused materials.

_____ I made an advertisement to sell my product.

_____ I used a (✓) to show what I included in my advertisement.

_____ I presented my advertisement to the class.

 Notes for Home: Your child learned how to make something new from something that has already been used.
Home Activity: With your child, look for items in your home that might be reused rather than discarded. Brainstorm toys, tools, or other things that your child might create with these items.

Workbook Discovery Channel Project **43**

Name _____ Date _____

Reading Social Studies
Use with Pages 204–205.

Cause and Effect

Directions: Often there are many reasons why an area has developed into the community it is today. Read the sentences that follow. Then use the strategy of cause and effect to answer the questions. Fill in the circle next to the correct answer.

1. Austin, Texas, has grown because of the technology companies located there. What caused Austin to grow?
   Ⓐ all companies
   Ⓑ technology companies
   Ⓒ ranches
   Ⓓ oil companies

2. Little Rock, Arkansas, began as a post on the Arkansas River. What was the effect of having a post on the river?
   Ⓐ The Arkansas River became a tourist attraction.
   Ⓑ More restaurants were built.
   Ⓒ Fewer boats came to Little Rock.
   Ⓓ Little Rock grew into a larger community.

3. The fur trade brought many people to Chicago, Illinois. What caused Chicago to grow into an important city?
   Ⓐ hunting
   Ⓑ fur trading
   Ⓒ shipping
   Ⓓ farming

4. Many immigrants who entered at Ellis Island stayed in New York City. What effect do you think Ellis Island had on New York City?
   Ⓐ The population increased.
   Ⓑ Trade increased.
   Ⓒ The population decreased.
   Ⓓ Trade decreased.

Notes for Home: Your child learned to use the strategy of cause and effect when reading.
Home Activity: How much do you and your child know about the history of your community? Work together to find out what caused its founders to establish it and what has helped it grow.

Name _____ Date _____

Vocabulary Preview

Use with Chapter 7.

Vocabulary Preview

Directions: You may be familiar with many of the terms you are learning in social studies. How much do you know about these words from Chapter 7? Write the number of each word on the scale below. Then write the definition of each word on the lines provided. You may use your glossary.

I know	**I have seen**	**I do not know**

1. explorer

   _____
   _____

2. fleet

   _____
   _____

3. fortification

   _____
   _____

4. representative government

   _____
   _____
   _____

Notes for Home: Your child learned the vocabulary terms for Chapter 7.
Home Activity: Research and discuss with your child who the explorers and settlers of your community were. Find out why your community grew in its present location.

Workbook

Vocabulary Preview **45**

Name _____ Date _____

Lesson Review
Use with Pages 208–211.

Lesson 1: Explorers Come to North America

Directions: When European explorers arrived in North America, they found the Iroquois already living there. Complete the outline with information from this lesson. You may use your textbook.

Explorers Come to North America

I. The Iroquois

    A. Lived in what is now _____ and _____

    B. The Iroquois set up a _____.

        1. They had a set of rules that protected _____ _____.

        2. The government also protected _____.

    C. Differences in customs and ideas led to _____.

II. Early Explorers

    A. Portugal, Spain, France, and England all traded for goods from _____ and _____.

        1. Traveling to China and India by _____ took a long time.

        2. Explorers wanted to find a _____ route.

    B. _____ led the way by sailing to the East around Africa.

    C. Some of Spain's explorers built settlements in _____.

    D. The _____ settled in present-day Canada.

    E. The _____ hoped to catch up with Spain and France.

Notes for Home: Your child learned about the Iroquois people and the first Europeans who came to North America.
Home Activity: Where is your family's country of origin? Discuss with your child how your family first came to the United States.

Name _____ Date _____

Research and Writing Skills
Use with Pages 212–213.

Use the Library

Directions: Suppose that your teacher asks you to prepare a report on the life of an Iroquois child. How will you research information for the assignment? Use what you learned about resources in a library to answer the questions that follow. You may use your textbook.

1. What kind of information will your classmates find interesting about the topic?

   _____
   _____
   _____

2. What types of reference books will be helpful to use? Why?

   _____
   _____
   _____

3. Should you use more than one or two sources for information? Why?

   _____
   _____
   _____

4. Will you use the Internet? If so, what keywords might help in your search?

   _____
   _____
   _____

Notes for Home: Your child learned how to use the library to research information for a given topic.
Home Activity: Visit a library with your child. Discuss with the library staff the variety of reference materials—print, visual, or online—that are available there.

Workbook   Research and Writing Skills   **47**

Name _____ Date _____ **Lesson Review**

Use with Pages 214–219.

Lesson 2: A Spanish Community

Directions: Early Spanish explorers spent much time setting up communities in the area that is now Florida. Complete the chart with information from this lesson. You may use your textbook.

Who?	Where?	What Is Important About Them or Their Area?
Ponce de León		
The French		
King Philip II		
Menéndez		
Kevin		

Notes for Home: Your child learned about early Spanish settlements in Florida.
Home Activity: In Spanish, the word *Florida* means "land of flowers." Discuss with your child what the Spanish explorers might have seen and how they might have felt when they arrived in Florida.

48 Lesson Review   Workbook

Name _____ Date _____

Map and Globe Skills
Use with Pages 222–223.

Use a Locator Map

Directions: A locator map can help you figure out where a particular place is located. Use what you learned about using a locator map to answer the questions that follow. Use complete sentences.

1. What is the first thing you should look for when you use a locator map?

   _____
   _____
   _____

2. What is the second thing to look for when you use a locator map?

   _____
   _____
   _____

3. What does the box, circle, shading, or symbol on a locator map tell you?

   _____
   _____
   _____

Notes for Home: Your child learned how to use locator maps.
Home Activity: Discuss the concept of "looking at the big picture" with your child. How does looking at the big picture help you make decisions at home or at work? How important is it as an adult to understand the need for looking at the big picture?

Name _____ Date _____

Lesson Review
Use with Pages 224–227.

Lesson 3: A French Community

Directions: The French established many communities in present-day Canada. Circle the term in parentheses that best completes each sentence with information from this lesson. You may use your textbook.

1. (Portugal, Britain) found a water route to the East.

2. In 1534 (Jacques Cartier, Samuel de Champlain) landed on the coast of present-day Newfoundland.

3. Rapids and waterfalls blocked Cartier's path (west, north).

4. In 1608 Samuel de Champlain found an Iroquois village called (Newfoundland, Stadacona).

5. Champlain built a French settlement called (Cartier, Quebec City).

6. In 1759 the (English, Spanish) defeated the French for rule over Canada.

7. (Old Quebec, Marie) is the area where the French built their fort.

8. Le Chateau Frontenac is a (fortification, hotel) in Old Quebec.

9. Musicians, jugglers, and artists entertain people in the (park, river) in the middle of the old part of the city.

10. French customs, traditions, and language are celebrated in Quebec (all year long, on special holidays).

Notes for Home: Your child learned about the French settlement of Quebec City.
Home Activity: Many people in Quebec City today speak French. What groups settled first in your area? Are the languages of these groups still spoken in your area?

Name _____ Date _____

Lesson Review
Use with Pages 230–235.

Lesson 4: An English Community

Directions: The English built their many communities in what is now the state of Virginia. Put the events below in the order they happened. Which event happened first? Write the number 1 on the line beside that event. Continue numbering the events from 2 to 12. You may use your textbook.

_____ The first representative assembly met in Jamestown.

_____ The first English settlers arrived in present-day Jamestown.

_____ John Smith had to return to England.

_____ The English settlers began running out of food.

_____ The Native Americans in Virginia planted crops and built villages.

_____ About four hundred new settlers arrived in Jamestown with supplies.

_____ Powhatan agreed to help the English settlers.

_____ Jamestown became a national historic site.

_____ Fire destroyed most of Jamestown.

_____ John Smith discovered that many of the settlers in Jamestown had died.

_____ John Smith led a search to find more food.

_____ The people of Jamestown lived through "the starving time."

Notes for Home: Your child learned about the English settlement of Jamestown.
Home Activity: Your child may be familiar with the story of Jamestown from the story or movie *Pocahontas*. Discuss with your child the differences between a movie and actual events in history.

Name _____ Date _____

> **Vocabulary Review**
> Use with Chapter 7.

Vocabulary Review

Directions: The words in the box are the vocabulary words from Chapter 7. Write a story on the lines below using all of these words. You may use your glossary.

| explorer | fleet | fortification | representative government |

_____
_____
_____
_____
_____
_____
_____
_____
_____
_____
_____
_____
_____

Notes for Home: Your child learned the vocabulary terms for Chapter 7.
Home Activity: Have your child write each word on four slips of paper. Write the definitions on four other slips. Turn papers written side down and shuffle. Together, match each word to its definition.

Name _____ Date _____

Vocabulary Preview
Use with Chapter 8.

Vocabulary Preview

Directions: The words in the box are the vocabulary words from Chapter 8. How much do you know about these words? Write the term that best answers each question on the lines provided. You may use your glossary.

Transcontinental Railroad	Morse code	pasteurization
Pony Express	broadcast	vaccine
invention	reaper	

1. Which of these is a weak or killed form of a disease that is given to people?
   _____

2. What linked the eastern United States to the West?
   _____

3. What was the system of delivering the mail on horseback called?
   _____

4. What series of telegraph signals stood for letters or words? _____

5. What is something that is made for the first time called? _____

6. Which is a machine that cuts grain? _____

7. Which is a process developed by Louis Pasteur? _____

8. What is another word for "sent out"? _____

Notes for Home: Your child learned the vocabulary terms for Chapter 8.
Home Activity: Your child may already be familiar with the terms *vaccine* and *invention*. Discuss examples of new discoveries with your child.

Name _____ Date _____

Lesson Review
Use with Pages 242–247.

Lesson 1: Transportation Over Time

Directions: Transportation has taken many forms throughout history. Complete the chart with information from this lesson. You may use your textbook.

How?	Who?	Where?	When?
Boat			
Foot			
Horseback			
Covered wagons			
Train (steam locomotive)			
Car			
Airplane			

Notes for Home: Your child learned about the history of many forms of transportation.
Home Activity: Which of the modes of transportation from the chart have you used? Discuss the advantages and disadvantages of them with your child.

Name _____ Date _____

Chart and Graph Skills
Use with Pages 248–249.

Use a Time Line

Directions: A time line shows when events occurred. Look at the time line that follows. It shows many important events in the history of transportation. Use it to answer the questions below.

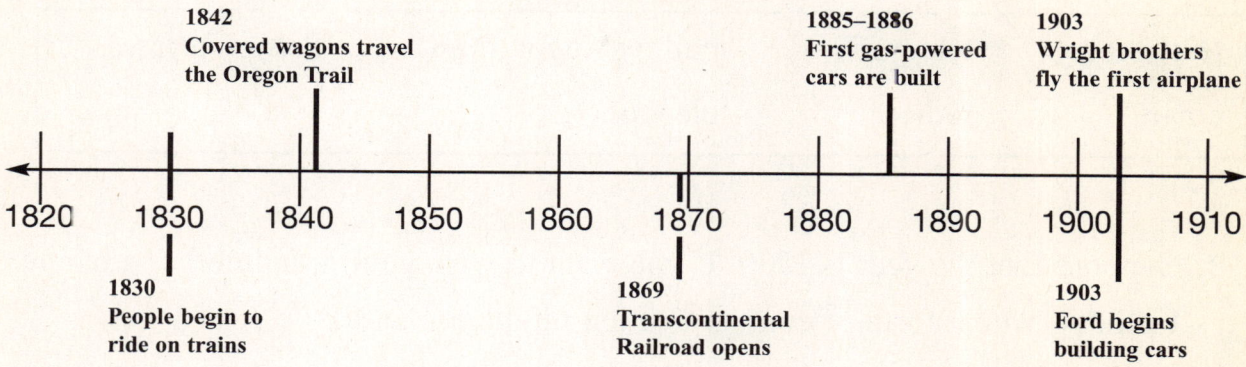

1. This time line is divided into groups of 10 years. What is another name for a period of 10 years? _____

2. Which event happened before covered wagons traveled on the Oregon Trail?
   _____

3. Which two key transportation events happened in 1903?
   _____ and _____

4. Which came first: the Transcontinental Railroad or the gas-powered car?
   _____

5. How long after the first gas-powered car was built did Ford start building cars?
   _____

Notes for Home: Your child learned how to use a time line.
Home Activity: Work with your child to make a simple time line of his or her life. Include important events such as birth, cutting the first tooth, birthdays, and starting school.

Workbook

Chart and Graph Skills **55**

Name _____ Date _____

Lesson Review
Use with Pages 250–255.

Lesson 2: Communication Over Time

Directions: People from around the world are able to keep in touch thanks to many types of communication. Use the forms of communication in the box to answer the questions that follow. You may use your textbook.

| television | telegraph | mail by wagon train | Pony Express |
| email | radio | telephone | |

1. Suppose that the year is 1789. If you want to wish your grandmother a happy birthday, which form of communication might you use?
   _____

2. Suppose that the year is 1861. If you want to say "Hello" to your friends in the East, which two forms of communication would be the best to use?
   _____ and _____ Which is faster?
   _____

3. Suppose that it is the late 1800s. Which form of communication would allow you to sing a song to your aunt who lives in the West?
   _____

4. Suppose that it is the early 1900s. Which form of communication would allow you and your family to enjoy listening to a program?
   _____

5. Suppose that the year is 1949. Which form of communication would bring the news of the world into your home? _____

6. Suppose that the year is 2003. Which form of communication would you use to send a letter to your teacher in just seconds? _____

Notes for Home: Your child learned how communication has changed through time.
Home Activity: Choose a family member or friend who lives in another community. Discuss with your child different ways to communicate with that person.

Name _____ Date _____

Lesson Review
Use with Pages 258–263.

Lesson 3: Inventions Over Time

Directions: Many inventions have made life easier. Circle the term in parentheses that best completes each sentence with information from this lesson. You may use your textbook.

1. Before the light bulb was invented, people used (candles, windows) to see at night.

2. Thomas Edison invented the (light bulb, telephone).

3. (Cyrus Hall McCormick, Lewis Latimer) was a famous African American inventor.

4. Latimer made special drawings of a (telephone, telegraph) for Alexander Graham Bell.

5. In the 1700s and 1800s, many people worked (on farms, in cities).

6. The (light bulb, reaper) is a machine that cuts grain to help farmers harvest crops.

7. Two men, Louis Daguerre and (Thomas Edison, George Eastman), invented ways for people to take and develop pictures.

8. DVDs and CDs have been developed over the last (20, 75) years.

Directions: In the space below, draw a picture of an invention that has made your life easier.

Notes for Home: Your child learned the histories of some important inventions.
Home Activity: Discuss with your child the effects of the invention of the light bulb. How dark would it be in your home without electric lights?

Workbook   Lesson Review **57**

Name _____ Date _____
Use with Pages 264–265.

Writing Prompt: Newspapers

Newspapers were popular during colonial times. They helped people learn about what was happening. Today, newspapers are widely read in the United States and around the world. Draw a picture of two places you can get a newspaper. Write about the different kinds of information you can find in a newspaper.

_____
_____
_____
_____

Notes for Home: Your child learned about communication in colonial times.
Home Activity: Look through a newspaper with your child. Discuss the different types of informatiion it contains, such as world and community news, entertainment, financial information, items for sale, job listings, and weather.

Name _____ Date _____

Lesson Review
Use with Pages 266–269.

Lesson 4: Medicine Improves Over Time

Directions: Many doctors and scientists have worked to make it easier to stay healthy. Complete the diagram that follows. Write what each person did to improve health care. You may use your textbook.

Edward Jenner

Louis Pasteur

Pioneers in Health Care

Jonas Salk

Gertrude Elion

Notes for Home: Your child learned about important improvements in health care.
Home Activity: Discuss vaccines with your child. Which vaccinations has your child already had? What diseases or illnesses do they help prevent?

Workbook

Lesson Review **59**

Name _____ Date _____

Thinking Skills

Use with Pages 270–271.

Solve Problems

You read about improvements made to medicine over time in this chapter. Scientists used a problem-solving process to find solutions.

Directions: Read the sentences in the box below. Then write them on the lines next to the correct step in the problem-solving process.

> Edward Jenner gave patients a weak form of cowpox.
> A disease known as smallpox was killing millions of people.
> Edward Jenner decided that people who had cowpox did not get smallpox.
> Edward Jenner's vaccine prevented smallpox from killing people.
> Edward Jenner gathered information on why people get diseases.
> Edward Jenner made a list of possible reasons why only some people were getting smallpox.

Step 1: Identify a problem. _____

_____

Step 2: Gather information. _____

_____

Step 3: List and consider options. _____

_____

Step 4: Consider advantages and disadvantages. _____

_____

Step 5: Choose and try a solution. _____

_____

Step 6: Decide if the solution works. _____

_____

Notes for Home: Your child learned to use the problem-solving process to solve problems.
Home Activity: With your child, identify an issue at home or in the community. Discuss how to use the steps in the problem-solving process to resolve the issue.

60 Thinking Skills   Workbook

Name _____ Date _____

Vocabulary Review

Use with Chapter 8.

Vocabulary Review

Directions: Write the definition to each vocabulary word from Chapter 8 on the line. You may use your glossary.

1. Transcontinental Railroad _____

2. Pony Express _____

3. invention _____

4. Morse code _____

5. broadcast _____

6. reaper _____

7. pasteurization _____

8. vaccine _____

Notes for Home: Your child learned the vocabulary terms for Chapter 8.
Home Activity: Take turns with your child using each of the vocabulary words from Chapter 8 in a sentence.

Workbook   Vocabulary Review **61**

Name _____ Date _____

Use with Page 280.

UNIT 4 Project Making Tracks

Directions: In a group, create a presentation about traveling with one of the French explorers.

1. Group members are:

   _____   _____   _____

   _____   _____   _____

2. The explorer we chose is _____.

3. The route we chose is _____.

4. We made a travel brochure. The (✔) shows what we included in our brochure:

   ___ Title   ___ Pictures   ___ Travel schedule

   ___ Drawings ___ Map   ___ Travel plans

   ___ Descriptions of geographical features (mountains, lakes, rivers, valleys)

5. We wrote about our travel adventure.

   _____

   _____

✔ Checklist for Students

_____ We chose part of a route taken by a French explorer.

_____ We made a travel brochure.

_____ We used a (✔) to show what we included in our brochure.

_____ We wrote about an adventure along the route.

_____ We presented our travel brochure to the class.

Notes for Home: Your child learned about French explorers in North America.
Home Activity: With your child, research the early explorers of your community. What country did they represent? What was their reason for exploring the area where you live?

62 Discovery Channel Project   Workbook

Name _____ Date _____

Reading Social Studies
Use with Pages 286–287.

Sequence

Directions: Sequence is the order in which events take place. Read the passage that follows. Then use the strategy of sequence to answer the questions. Fill in the circle next to the correct answer.

Mary Kay Ash always has worked hard. As a child, she helped her mother with the housework and the cooking. She also helped take care of her sick father. Then she studied hard to be successful in high school.

After she married, she began her long career in sales. First she sold children's books. Next she sold housewares and cleaning supplies. Then in 1952, she began working for a giftware company.

Finally, in 1963, she started her own company. Its first product was a skin lotion. Today her company sells its many products around the world.

1. Which word in the first paragraph helps show sequence?
   Ⓐ then
   Ⓑ take
   Ⓒ always
   Ⓓ sick

2. Which did Mary Kay Ash do first?
   Ⓐ She sold cleaning products.
   Ⓑ She sold books.
   Ⓒ She started her own company.
   Ⓓ She went to high school.

3. What was the first product sold by Mary Kay Ash's own company?
   Ⓐ lotion
   Ⓑ supplies
   Ⓒ books
   Ⓓ housewares

Notes for Home: Your child learned to use the strategy of sequence when reading.
Home Activity: Discuss the major events of your life with your child. Write each on a piece of paper. Use clue words such as *first, second*, and *then* to help your child sequence the events.

Name _____ Date _____

Vocabulary Preview

Vocabulary Preview
Use with Chapter 9.

Directions: These are the vocabulary words from Chapter 9. How much do you know about these words? Write each word in the space provided beside its definition. Not all words will be used. You may use your glossary.

earn	spending	opportunity cost	product	profit
budget	saving	good	supply	
income	economic choice	service	demand	

1. _____ a plan that shows income, spending, and saving

2. _____ to get paid for working

3. _____ a good or a service

4. _____ the decision to buy one thing rather than another

5. _____ the income a business has left after all its costs are paid

6. _____ all the money a person earns from a job or other places

7. _____ a job that one person does for another person

8. _____ the amount of a product that producers want to sell at different prices

9. _____ something people make or grow and then sell

10. _____ the amount of income that is not spent

Notes for Home: Your child learned the vocabulary terms for Chapter 9.
Home Activity: Write a sentence for each of the terms above. Leave a blank where the term would be. Have your child try to fill in the missing term by analyzing the context of the sentence.

Name _____ Date _____

Lesson Review
Use with Pages 290–295.

Lesson 1: Earning, Spending, and Saving

Directions: Learning how to wisely earn, spend, and save money will help you throughout your life. Read the sample budget. Then answer the questions that follow. You may use your textbook.

MY BUDGET

Week	Earning	Spending	Saving
Week 1	$10.00	$5.00	$5.00
Week 2	$14.00	$3.00	$11.00
Week 3	$10.00	$5.00	$5.00
Week 4	$10.00	$2.00	$8.00
Total	$44.00	$15.00	$29.00

1. During which week did you earn the most money? _____

2. During which weeks did you spend the most money? _____

3. Suppose that you want to buy a basketball that costs $20.00. Do you have enough money saved after four weeks? _____ Can you also buy a CD that costs $12.00? _____

4. How much do you think you might earn during Week 5? _____ After Week 5 would you be able to buy both the basketball and the CD? _____

5. During which week did you save the most money? _____

6. During which week did you spend the least amount of money? _____

Notes for Home: Your child learned about earning, spending, and saving money.
Home Activity: Does your family follow a household budget? Discuss with your child what your family spends, on average, each week for groceries. Brainstorm ways to cut spending.

Name _____ Date _____

Use with Pages 296–297.

Writing Prompt: Money

People have used different forms of money for thousands of years. Today, people still use money to get the things they need or want. Draw a picture of things you can buy with money. Write about some ways money can help you meet your needs.

_____
_____
_____
_____

Notes for Home: Your child learned about different forms of money.
Home Activity: With your child, design a coin that he or she can earn and exchange for special privileges in your home. Cut a circle from cardboard and cover it with tinfoil. Then transfer your design to the coin using a capped ballpoint pen. Help your child transfer the design without tearing the foil.

Name _____ Date _____

Lesson Review
Use with Pages 300–303.

Lesson 2: Choosing Wisely

Directions: It is often difficult to choose between something you want and something you need. Answer the questions that follow about making economic choices. Use complete sentences. You may use your textbook.

1. Suppose that you have $40. You can buy either a baseball glove that costs $38 or a set of books that costs $35. Which will you buy? Why? What is your opportunity cost?

   _____
   _____
   _____

2. Suppose that you have $25. You are working to save money in a bank account. Should you buy a stuffed animal that costs $20? Why or why not?

   _____
   _____
   _____

3. Suppose that you have $30. You can buy a ticket to the state fair for a total of $15 or decide not to go. Is buying a ticket to the fair a want or a need? Will you spend the $15? Why or why not?

   _____
   _____
   _____

Notes for Home: Your child learned about making economic choices.
Home Activity: Take your child with you on your next trip to the grocery store. Discuss the economic choices you are making. Discuss sale prices, coupons, quality, and other factors that lead you to choose one product over another.

Workbook   Lesson Review **67**

Name _____ Date _____

Thinking Skills

Use with Pages 304–305.

Make a Decision

Directions: Following a step-by-step plan can help you make wise decisions. Complete the chart below with the five steps of the decision-making process from your textbook.

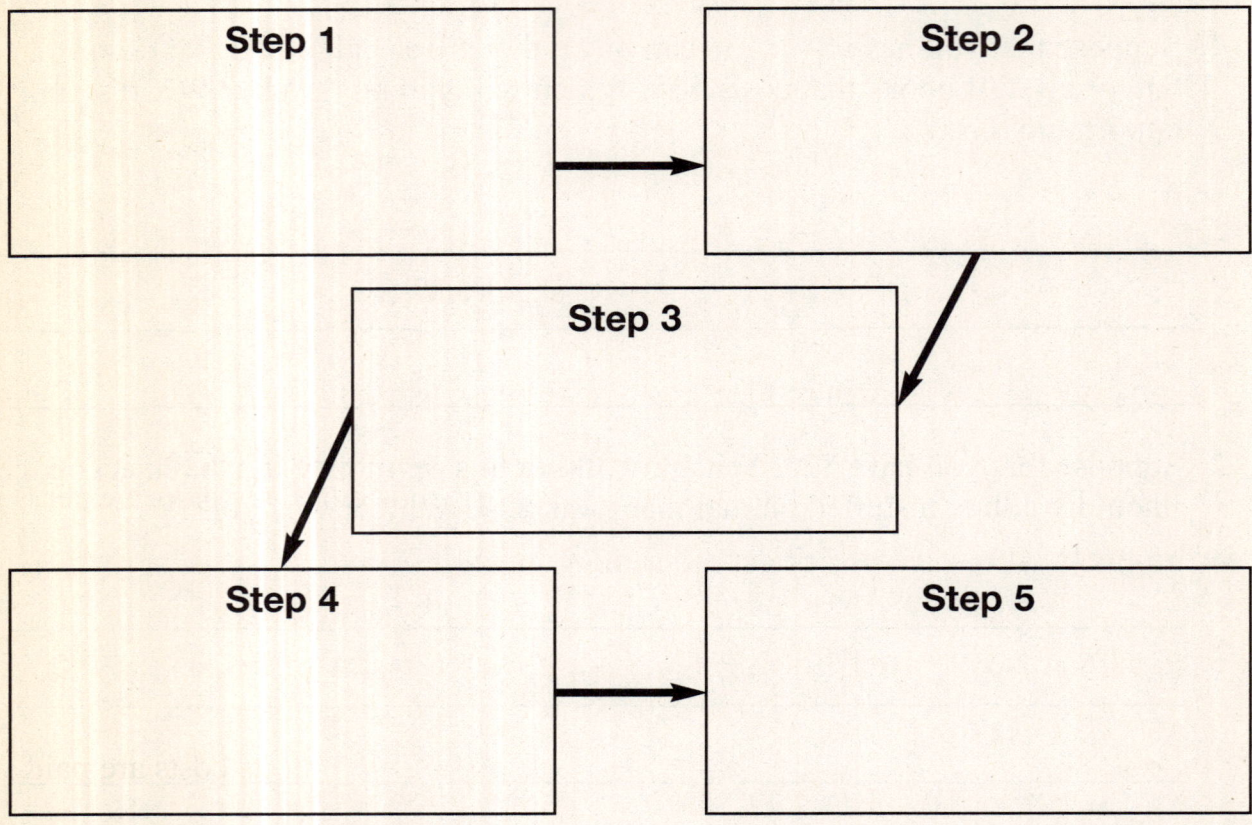

Directions: Think about a decision that you made recently. Did you use a step-by-step plan to make that decision? If so, do you think the plan helped you make a wise decision? If not, how might using a plan in the future help you make a wise decision?

_____
_____
_____
_____

 Notes for Home: Your child learned how to use a step-by-step plan to make a decision.
Home Activity: Discuss with your child a major decision you have made recently. Explain how following a step-by-step plan helps people make wise decisions.

Name _____ Date _____

Lesson Review

Use with Pages 306–311.

Lesson 3: A Community Business

Directions: There probably are many different businesses in or near your community. Each of these community businesses provides goods or services or both. Circle the term in parentheses that best completes each sentence with information from this lesson. You may use your textbook.

1. Softball bats, vegetables, and books are (goods, services).

2. An umpire provides a (good, service) at a softball game.

3. Goods and services together are called (bats, products).

4. If the supply of a certain product increases, the price usually will go (up, down).

5. If few people are buying bats from the sporting goods store, the store owner probably will (lower the price, order more bats).

6. Usually if the (demand, supply) for a product decreases, the price will go down.

7. Profit is the (income, supply) that a business has left after all its costs are paid.

8. To help it make a profit, a business will try to keep the cost of making goods (down, up).

9. A business can make a larger profit by selling its products at a (lower, higher) price.

10. When given a choice, people want to pay (less, more) for a product they want to buy.

Notes for Home: Your child learned about how businesses work to make a profit.
Home Activity: Discuss with your child different goods and services your family uses on a regular basis. Is there a business in your community that provides you with the majority of these products? Do any businesses provide you with both goods and services?

Workbook

Lesson Review **69**

Name _____ Date _____

Vocabulary Review

Use with Chapter 9.

Vocabulary Review

Directions: Fill in the circle next to the vocabulary term that best completes each sentence.

1. Baseball bats, softballs, and gloves are _____.
   - Ⓐ services
   - Ⓑ goods
   - Ⓒ profit

2. You can _____ money by working and getting paid.
   - Ⓐ earn
   - Ⓑ want
   - Ⓒ budget

3. Making a _____ can help you plan how to spend your money.
   - Ⓐ profit
   - Ⓑ demand
   - Ⓒ budget

4. Hair stylists, umpires, and doctors provide _____ to others in the community.
   - Ⓐ supplies
   - Ⓑ services
   - Ⓒ goods

5. Robin had to make an _____ between buying two CDs and buying a baseball bat.
   - Ⓐ opportunity cost
   - Ⓑ income
   - Ⓒ economic choice

6. Juan is _____ his money to use at a later time.
   - Ⓐ spending
   - Ⓑ income
   - Ⓒ saving

7. Goods and services together are called _____.
   - Ⓐ products
   - Ⓑ spending
   - Ⓒ profits

8. When the _____ for a product increases, its price often goes up.
   - Ⓐ demand
   - Ⓑ income
   - Ⓒ saving

9. Business owners work hard to keep their costs low so they can make a _____.
   - Ⓐ need
   - Ⓑ profit
   - Ⓒ supply

Notes for Home: Your child learned the vocabulary terms for Chapter 9.
Home Activity: Five of the vocabulary terms from this chapter were not used above. Take turns with your child using the terms *income, spending, saving, need,* and *supply* in sentences.

Name _____ Date _____

Vocabulary Preview

Directions: These are the vocabulary terms from Chapter 10. How much do you know about these terms? Write the number of the answer on the line provided. Not all words will be used. You may use your glossary.

1. renewable resource
2. nonrenewable resource
3. human resource
4. producer
5. specialize
6. capital resource
7. scarcity
8. interdependence
9. trade
10. communication
11. international trade
12. import
13. export
14. free market

____ a. trade between different countries

____ b. to send products and resources to other countries

____ c. a person who makes a product or provides a service

____ d. the sharing of information or news

____ e. to bring resources and other products from one country into another country

____ f. someone who makes products

____ g. to do one job or make one part of a product

____ h. a resource that can be replaced within a short time

____ i. a machine, tool, or building used to produce goods and services

____ j. when people choose what to produce and what to buy

____ k. to buy or sell goods and services

____ l. a resource that takes a long time to replace or cannot be replaced

Notes for Home: Your child learned the vocabulary terms for Chapter 10.
Home Activity: With your child, examine the words *import* and *export*. Point out the root *port* and the prefixes *im-* and *ex-*. What other words can you think of that use that root or those prefixes?

Name _____ Date _____

Lesson Review

Use with Pages 318–323.

Lesson 1: Using Resources

Direction: It takes many types of resources to make the products you use each day. Complete the chart that follows with information from this lesson. You may use your textbook.

Type of Resource	Examples	Products
Renewable		
Nonrenewable		
Human		
Capital		

Directions: In the space below, draw a type of product that comes from a renewable source.

Notes for Home: Your child learned how businesses use resources to make products.
Home Activity: Do you or does anyone in your family serve as a human resource for a business? Discuss with your child that person's role in making goods or providing services.

72 Lesson Review

Workbook

Name _____ Date _____

Chart and Graph Skills

Use with Pages 324–325.

Use a Cutaway Diagram

Maine lobsters are a renewable natural resource. People catch lobsters in a lobster pot, or cage. Then they ship the lobsters to markets across the country.

Directions: A cutaway diagram shows you what is inside of an object. Study the diagram of a lobster pot. Answer the questions on the lines provided.

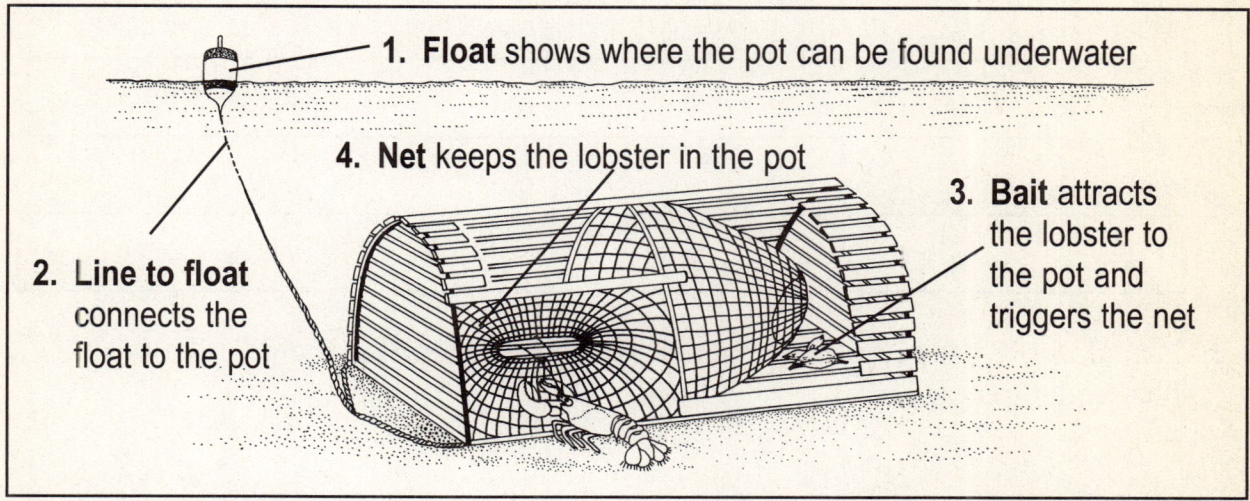

1. **Float** shows where the pot can be found underwater
2. **Line to float** connects the float to the pot
3. **Bait** attracts the lobster to the pot and triggers the net
4. **Net** keeps the lobster in the pot

1. Which two parts of the diagram show the inside of the lobster pot?

   _____

2. What part of the lobster pot would you look for to locate it underwater?

   _____

3. Why do you think bait attracts the lobster to the pot?

   _____

   _____

4. In catching a lobster, which step happens first: (4) *Net keeps the lobster in the pot* or (3) *Bait attracts the lobster to the pot and triggers the net*?

   _____

Notes for Home: Your child learned to interpret a cutaway diagram.
Home Activity: Brainstorm a list of objects in your home, such as a dishwasher or refrigerator, that could be drawn as a cutaway diagram. Discuss with your child the parts inside the object and how they work.

Name _____ Date _____

Lesson Review
Use with Pages 328–333.

Lesson 2: Depending on Others

Direction: People have to use their resources wisely. Use complete sentences to answer the questions that follow. You may use your textbook.

1. What is scarcity? Which resources are scarce?

   _____
   _____
   _____
   _____

2. Explain how the people of Phoenix, Arizona, depend on the people of Portland, Oregon.

   _____
   _____
   _____
   _____

3. What two resources were scarce in Robin's community? What choices did her community make? What work did people do to solve their scarcity problems?

   _____
   _____
   _____
   _____
   _____

Notes for Home: Your child learned how scarcity of resources affects communities.
Home Activity: Discuss the concepts of scarcity and conservation with your child. Stress the importance of making wise choices when using resources.

Name _____ Date _____

Lesson Review
Use with Pages 334–339.

Lesson 3: A World of Trade

Directions: People around the world depend on each other for goods and services. Use the terms in the box to complete each sentence with information from this lesson. You will use each term once. You may use your textbook.

| computers | communication | money | exported | traded |
| transportation | government | free | trucks | |

1. Two reasons why people around the world can depend on each other are _____ and _____.

2. People use airplanes, trains, ships, and _____ to move goods.

3. People now use phones and _____ to communicate instantly around the world.

4. Long ago people _____ the goods they produced for goods that they could not produce themselves.

5. Today people usually trade goods and services for _____.

6. Computers, airplanes, and other products are _____ from the United States to other countries.

7. In the United States people and companies are a part of a _____ market.

8. In some countries the _____ decides what is bought and sold.

Notes for Home: Your child learned how communities around the world depend on each other.
Home Activity: Look through your kitchen pantry or refrigerator with your child. Examine the labels on a number of products to see if they were imported from other countries. If resources are available, locate those countries on a world map or globe.

Workbook   Lesson Review **75**

Name _____ Date _____

Vocabulary Review
Use with Chapter 10.

Vocabulary Review

Directions: Write each word in the space provided beside its definition. Not all words will be used.

renewable resource	specialize	trade	export
nonrenewable resource	capital resource	communication	free market
human resource	scarcity	international trade	
producer	interdependence	import	

1. _____ there is not enough of something to meet all of people's wants and needs

2. _____ a machine, tool, or building that is used to produce goods and services

3. _____ someone who makes products

4. _____ a resource that takes a long time to replace or cannot be replaced

5. _____ trade between different countries

6. _____ to bring products and resources from one country into another country

7. _____ a resource that can be replaced quickly

8. _____ the sharing of information or news

9. _____ when people choose what to produce and buy

10. _____ to do one job or make one part of a product

Notes for Home: Your child learned the vocabulary terms for Chapter 10.
Home Activity: Select a service or product, such as computers. Then take turns with your child using the vocabulary terms in sentences related to the product you choose.

76 Vocabulary Review

Workbook

Name _____ Date _____

Use with Page 348.

Unit 5 Project   On the Market

Directions: In a group, create an advertisement for goods or a service that you think is important.

1. Group members are:

   _____   _____

   _____   _____

2. The goods or service we will advertise is _____.

3. We chose to advertise these goods or service because _____
   _____.

4. We made an advertisement for our goods or service. The (✔) shows what we included:

   ____ Name of the goods or service

   ____ Pictures of the goods or service

   ____ Price

   ____ Why people should buy or use it

✔ **Checklist for Students**

____ We chose goods or a service.

____ We made an advertisement to market our goods or service.

____ We used a (✔) to show what we included in our advertisement.

____ We presented our advertisement to the class.

Notes for Home: Students learned about goods and services provided to communities.
Home Activity: With your child, study the Yellow Pages of a local-area telephone book. Tally the number of businesses that advertise goods to your community and the number that offer services. Which is greater?

Workbook   Discovery Channel Project **77**

Name _____ Date _____

Reading Social Studies
Use with Pages 354–355.

Summarize

A summary must include two important things: the main idea of the passage and the important details.

Directions: Read the passage that follows. Then use the strategy of summarizing to answer the questions. Fill in the circle next to the correct answer.

You may think that being a part of local government is only for older people. However, some very young citizens have shown that they can help too.

The youngest person ever to hold the office of mayor in the United States was Shane Mack. He was elected in 1988 when he was only 18 years old. He served for eight years as the mayor of his hometown, Castlewood, South Dakota. More recently, in March of 1999, Jason Nastke was elected as mayor of Valatie, New York. He was only 19 years old when voted into office. Another New York community, Tivoli, also had a teenage mayor. Marc Molinaro was elected in 1995 at age 19.

Citizens often vote for young candidates because of their new ideas. But these young mayors still have to prove themselves. Like any other elected officials, these individuals have to do what they promise the voters in order to be chosen again in the next election.

1. What is the main idea of this passage?
   Ⓐ Only older people can help in local government.
   Ⓑ Elected officials have to do what they promise voters.
   Ⓒ Young people can be an important part of local government.
   Ⓓ You have to be at least 19 years old to be an elected mayor.

2. Which detail does NOT support the passage's main idea?
   Ⓐ Shane Mack was elected mayor at the age of 18.
   Ⓑ Young mayors still have to prove themselves.
   Ⓒ The mayor of Valatie, New York, is only 19 years old.
   Ⓓ Marc Molinaro served as the mayor of Tivoli, New York, at age 19.

Notes for Home: Your child learned to use the strategy of summarizing.
Home Activity: Discuss with your child the young mayors from the passage. Why do you think they ran for office at such a young age? What local issues might be most important to a young politician?

Name _____ Date _____

Vocabulary Preview

Vocabulary Preview
Use with Chapter 11.

Directions: These are the vocabulary words from Chapter 11. How much do you know about these words? Write each word in the space provided beside its definition. You may use your glossary.

| direct democracy | republic | amendment | responsibility |

1. _____ a change

2. _____ a government in which citizens elect representatives to speak for them

3. _____ a government that is run by the citizens who live under it

4. _____ a duty, something you should do

Directions: Use each word in a sentence. Write each sentence on the lines provided below.

5. _____

6. _____

7. _____

8. _____

Notes for Home: Your child learned the vocabulary terms for Chapter 11.
Home Activity: Scramble the letters of each vocabulary word above. Have your child unscramble the letters to reveal the vocabulary for this chapter.

Workbook   Vocabulary Preview **79**

Name _____ Date _____

Lesson Review
Use with Pages 358–361.

Lesson 1: Governments in the Past

Directions: The founders of the United States were influenced by governments of the past. Use complete sentences to answer the questions that follow. You may use your textbook.

1. Why did people long ago form communities?

   _____
   _____
   _____

2. What kind of government did the citizens of Athens, Greece, live under?

   _____
   _____
   _____

3. What type of government do we live under in the United States?

   _____
   _____
   _____

4. Why did the *Mayflower* colonists leave England?

   _____
   _____
   _____

5. What was the Mayflower Compact? What did it say?

   _____
   _____
   _____
   _____

Notes for Home: Your child learned about governments in the past.
Home Activity: What are the benefits of living in a republic? What are possible disadvantages? With your child, relate these ideas to our form of government in the United States.

80 Lesson Review   Workbook

Name _____ Date _____

Thinking Skills

Use with Pages 362–363.

Identify Point of View

Directions: Identifying different points of view can help you understand why people disagree. Read the passage that follows. Then use complete sentences to answer the questions.

Suppose that your school is considering having students wear uniforms. Many people have given their opinions on this issue. There are many points of view.

Your principal would like students and teachers to wear uniforms. She feels that the uniforms would help students focus on their work. Many teachers want students to wear uniforms but feel that teachers should not have to. Your gym teacher thinks it would take too much time in gym class for students to change out of and back into their uniforms. Some parents believe that it would cost too much to buy uniforms. Other parents think uniforms would be cheaper than other types of clothes.

1. Why does the principal want students and teachers to wear uniforms?

   _____

   _____

2. Why does the gym teacher not want students to wear uniforms?

   _____

   _____

3. What is your point of view about school uniforms?

   _____

   _____

Notes for Home: Your child learned how to identify points of view.
Home Activity: Discuss with your child his or her point of view about school uniforms. How do you feel about them as a parent?

Name _____ Date _____

Lesson Review
Use with Pages 366–371.

Lesson 2: United States Government

Directions: Many people helped shape the government we have today in the United States. Complete the boxes below with important information about each person. You may use your textbook.

Thomas Jefferson

George Washington

Freedom

Rosa Parks

Thurgood Marshall

Notes for Home: Your child learned about the United States government.
Home Activity: Discuss with your child any amendments to the U.S. Constitution with which you are familiar, such as the First Amendment or the Fifth Amendment. How are these amendments important to you and your family?

Name _____ Date _____

Use with Pages 374–375.

Writing Prompt: Good Citizens

In 1787, American leaders met in Philadelphia to make a new government. They practiced good citizenship by taking responsibility for the future of their community. What are some ways you can be a good citizen? Draw a picture of yourself practicing good citizenship. Write about what you would do.

_____
_____
_____
_____

Notes for Home: Your child learned about early American leaders.
Home Activity: With your child, discuss how the Virginia representatives showed that they were good citizens. Ask your child how these actions affected others. Brainstorm ways that your family can benefit others by being good citizens.

Workbook   Writing Prompt **83**

Name _____ Date _____

Lesson Review
Use with Pages 376–379.

Lesson 3: Being a Good Citizen

Directions: A good citizen understands that having rights also means having responsibilities. Complete the outline with information from this lesson. You may use your textbook.

Responsibilities of a Good Citizen

I. Respect the _____ and _____ of others.

II. Obey the _____ of your country and your community.

III. Pay _____.

IV. Help _____ your country and your community.

V. _____ to elect leaders.

  A. _____ to the people who want to be elected.

  B. Decide who would be the _____ person for the job.

  C. Then you _____ for the candidate you have selected.

VI. Volunteer in the community.

  A. Help people who are _____.

  B. Help people who need _____.

Notes for Home: Your child learned about how to be a good citizen.
Home Activity: Discuss with your child what you do as a good citizen of your community. Together, brainstorm ways to become an even better citizen.

Name _____ Date _____ **Vocabulary Review**

Use with Chapter 11.

Vocabulary Review

Directions: Use the vocabulary words in the box to complete each sentence. Then write the definition of the word on the lines provided.

| direct democracy | republic | amendment | responsibility |

1. The government of Athens, Greece, was a _____.

   _____
   _____

2. An _____ to the Constitution can be found in the Bill of Rights.

   _____
   _____

3. Voting is an example of an important _____.

   _____
   _____

4. The government of the United States is a _____.

   _____
   _____

Notes for Home: Your child learned the vocabulary terms for Chapter 11.
Home Activity: Discuss the term *responsibility* with your child. Does your child have any responsibilities in your family, such as doing chores or homework? What happens when someone does not live up to his or her responsibilities?

Name _____ Date _____

Vocabulary Preview

Vocabulary Preview
Use with Chapter 12.

Directions: These are the vocabulary words from Chapter 12. How much do you know about these words? Draw a line from each word to its meaning. You may use your glossary.

1. recreation
2. council
3. mayor
4. candidate
5. consent
6. veto

a. a group of people who make laws and rules for a community
b. when a governor does not approve a bill
c. a person who runs for office
d. a way of enjoying yourself
e. the leader of a community
f. permission

Directions: Write a paragraph using all the vocabulary words shown above. Write the paragraph on the lines provided.

_____
_____
_____
_____
_____
_____
_____

Notes for Home: Your child learned the vocabulary terms for Chapter 12.
Home Activity: Review your child's paragraph. Did he or she use the vocabulary terms correctly? Did he or she use correct punctuation and capitalization? Help your child edit and improve the paragraph.

Name _____ Date _____

Lesson Review
Use with Pages 384–387.

Lesson 1: Community Services

Directions: Local governments provide many services for their citizens. Complete the chart with information from this lesson. You may use your textbook.

Type of Service	How Is It Provided by Local Governments?
Safety	
Education	
Recreation	
Transportation	

Notes for Home: Your child learned about the services local governments provide to their citizens.
Home Activity: Discuss with your child how your community meets your family's needs for safety, education, recreation, and transportation.

Workbook

Lesson Review **87**

Name _____ Date _____

Map and Globe Skills

Use with Pages 388–389.

Understand Latitude and Longitude

Directions: People use latitude and longitude to find exact places, or "addresses," on maps. Use the map below to answer the questions on this page.

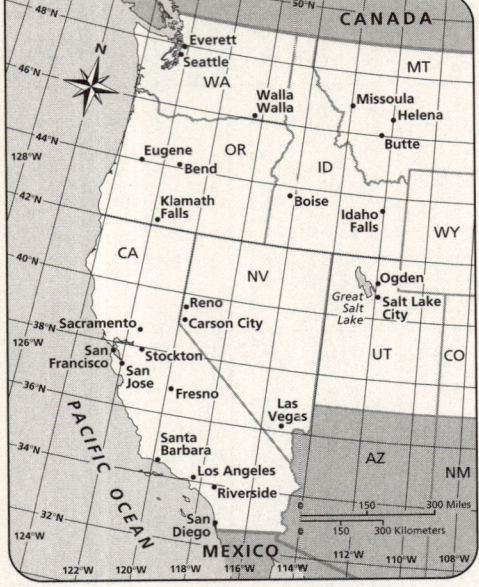

1. Which latitude line forms the boundary of three states on the map?

   _____

2. Which longitude line runs through four cities on the map?

   _____

3. What city on the map is closest to 48° N, 122° W?

   _____

4. What is the closest address for Walla Walla?

   _____

5. Which two cities are closest to 34° N, 118° W?

   _____

Notes for Home: Your child learned how to read latitude and longitude lines on a map.
Home Activity: Discuss latitude and longitude with your child. Use a map or globe, if available. Explain that latitude and longitude form a grid on a map or globe. Call out specific intersections of latitude and longitude, and have your child identify what is found there.

88 Lesson Review

Map and Globe Skills

Name _____ Date _____ | **Lesson Review**
Use with Pages 390–395.

Lesson 2: Community Leaders

Direction: Many people work together to help a community meet its needs. Circle the term in parentheses that best completes each sentence with information from this lesson. You may use your textbook.

1. The adults in your community pick local leaders by (voting, protesting).

2. A (town, council) is a group of people who make laws and rules for a community.

3. A (chief, mayor) is the leader of a community.

4. The (fire chief, council) runs the fire department.

5. Before becoming a member of a city council, a candidate must be chosen by the (mayor, people).

6. (Candidates, Citizens) explain what they would do to help the community if elected.

7. On (New Year's Day, Election Day), people vote for the candidates they think will be best for the community.

8. People want the leaders they elect to make and carry out (laws, governments).

9. People give their (consent, election) to leaders to carry out laws.

10. Leaders and citizens who (ignore, obey) laws help the community and its government work smoothly.

Notes for Home: Your child learned how certain people lead their communities.
Home Activity: Discuss with your child your local government. Who are its leaders? Do you have a city or town council? How are the police and fire chiefs chosen?

Name _____ Date _____

Lesson Review
Use with Pages 398–401.

Lesson 3: State Government

Directions: Fill in the chart below with the branches of state government, members of each branch, and examples of their responsibilites.

Branch	Members	Responsibilities

Notes for Home: Your child learned about the state government and how it provides many important services.
Home Activity: Review your child's chart above. Discuss with your child how government leaders in each branch of government work together to make your state a better place to live.

Name _____ Date _____

Vocabulary Review

Use with Chapter 12.

Vocabulary Review

Directions: Use the clues from the chapter to complete the puzzle.

| recreation | mayor | consent |
| council | candidate | veto |

Across

1. a way of enjoying yourself

2. People give their _____ to elected officials to make and carry out laws.

3. a person who runs for office

Down

1. the leader of a community

2. When a governor does not approve a bill

3. The mayor and the town _____ work together to run the community.

 **Notes for Home:** Your child learned the vocabulary terms for Chapter 12
Home Activity: Take turns with your child using the vocabulary terms above in sentences.

Name _____ Date _____

Use with Page 410.

UNIT 6 Project   Next Question!

Directions: Hold a press conference in your class. Each student will play the role of a local government leader or news reporter. Ask the government leaders questions about your community.

1. We chose these local government leaders to interview:

   _____ _____ _____

2. The (✔) shows the role I will play:

   ___ Government leader   ___ News reporter

3. This is how I prepared for my role:

Government Leader

- I made an official name tag. The (✔) shows what I included on my name tag:

   ___ My name   ___ My title

- My job as a government leader is to _____.

News Reporter

- I made a press pass. The (✔) shows what I included on my press pass:

   ___ My name   ___ My title   ___ Group I represent

✔ **Checklist for Students**

___ I helped choose which government leaders to interview.
___ I used a (✔) to show what role I will play.
___ I used a (✔) to show how I prepared for my role.
___ I participated in the press conference.

Notes for Home: Your child learned about local government leaders and the services they provide to a community.
Home Activity: With your child, make a directory of local government leaders, their responsibilities, and their telephone numbers. Tape your directory to your telephone book for easy reference.